DEVELOPING

TRANSACTIONAL ANALYSIS
COUNSELLING

Developing Counselling, edited by Windy Dryden, is an innovative series of books which provides counsellors and counselling trainees with practical hints and guidelines on the problems they face in the counselling process. The books assume that readers have a working knowledge of the approach in question and, in a clear and accessible fashion, show how the counsellor can more effectively translate that knowledge into everyday practice.

Books in the series include:

Developing the Practice of Counselling
Windy Dryden and Colin Feltham

Developing Counsellor Supervision
Colin Feltham and Windy Dryden

Developing Counsellor Training
Windy Dryden and Colin Feltham

Developing Person-Centred Counselling
Dave Mearns

Developing Psychodynamic Counselling
Brendan McLoughlin

Developing Rational Emotive Behavioural Counselling
Windy Dryden and Joseph Yankura

Developing Cognitive-Behavioural Counselling
Michael J. Scott, Stephen G. Stradling and Windy Dryden

DEVELOPING TRANSACTIONAL ANALYSIS COUNSELLING

Ian Stewart

SAGE Publications
London ● Thousand Oaks ● New Delhi

First published 1996
Reprinted 2006

SAGE Publications Ltd
1 Oliver's Yard, 55 City Road
London EC1Y 1SP

SAGE Publications Inc
2455 Teller Road
Thousand Oaks, California 91320

SAGE Publications India Pvt Ltd.
B-42 Panchsheel Enclave
Post Box 4109
New Delhi 110 017

British Library Cataloguing in Publication data

A catalogue record for this book is
available from the British Library
   ISBN-10 0 8039 7901 0
   ISBN-10 0 8039 7902 9 (pbk)
   ISBN-13 978 0 8039 7901 7 (hbk)
   ISBN-13 978 0 8039 7902 4 (pbk)
Library of Congress catalog record available

Typeset by Mayhew Typesetting, Rhayader, Powys
Printed and bound by Athenaeum Press Ltd., Gateshead, Tyne & Wear

Contents

Preface   vii

I   *Principles of TA*   1

An Outline of TA Theory   3

Principles of TA Treatment   13

II   *Thirty Ways to Develop your TA Counselling*   21

First Principles   23

  1   Presuppose the 'one-session cure'   23

  2   Stay aware of time-frames   27

  3   Line up the row of dominoes   34

  4   Set clear and flexible boundaries   38

  5   Ask your client to draw up a goals list   43

  6   Analyse life-script with a brief questionnaire   48

  7   Invite your client to close escape hatches –
non-routinely   54

  8   Keep your case notes as a 'front sheet'   59

Contract-making   65

  9   Distinguish contracts from outcomes and actions   66

10   Keep track of multiple outcomes: the Outcome Matrix   71

11   Ensure that the contract is sensory-based   78

12   Invite contracts that are finishable   83

13   Agree markers for script change   87

14   Keep the contract clear and flexible   93

15   Put the contract in context   97

16   Bring the contract alive through visualisation   102

Using the Process Model   109

17   Be a skilled 'driver detective'   109

18   Avoid inviting drivers   117

19   Recognise the six personality adaptations   122

20   Confront the process script   130

21   Make and keep contact: the Ware Sequence   137

22   Get on your client's wavelength: the five Channels of
     communication   142

23   Bring it all together: the complete Process Model   148

24   As your client moves on the Process Model, move
     with her   159

Treatment Tactics   165

25   Encourage discomfort and confusion   165

26   Know what and when to confront   171

27   Confront softly   175

28   Keep script insights in the past where they belong   180

29   Deal with voices in the head   184

30   If you split people, get them back together   191

Afterword: Living the Therapeutic Relationship   197

References   205

Index   207

Preface

In this book, I offer you 30 practical suggestions on how to develop your effectiveness in using transactional analysis (TA).

I am assuming that you already know the basics of TA, and that you want now to expand your skills in using it in counselling or psychotherapy. I assume too that you are already seeing clients, or that you are actively in training to do so.

While TA provides the book's core model, you will find much of the material immediately useful even if you work mainly within another approach. The section in Part II on 'Contract-making' offers ways to enhance contractual work in any modality. The Process Model, also described in Part II, provides a powerful system for client assessment and treatment planning that is equally effective inside or outside TA.

New material in this book

Like all the authors in the *Developing Counselling* series, I was briefed by the series editor to consider especially the needs of the newer counsellor. Also, I was to focus on helping people 'avoid common errors'. I set out to choose my 30 suggestions with that in mind, feeling slightly apprehensive that I might end up ploughing through old-hat accepted wisdom.

As I planned the book, however, I was surprised to realise that the information I was choosing for the 30 hints was *not* standard, run-of-the-mill stuff. Far from it: most of it is new. Much of the material in Part II is appearing here for the first time in book form. Some of the 30 suggestions have never been published before, while others have appeared only in the professional TA journal literature. Still others are well-established in neuro-linguistic programming (NLP) but have not been applied to TA until now.

It seemed odd to me at first to realise that I was writing mainly about new material, while at the same time addressing 'common errors'. But on thinking about it further, I realised that this is not paradoxical at all. Why should certain errors be 'common errors'?

Because the literature available until now has given little guidance on how to avoid them. I hope this book will help remedy that.

This is the only book at present in which you will find the material on the *Process Model* (Points 17–24) applied to counselling and psychotherapy[1]. The suggestions on the use of time-frames and verb tenses (Points 2, 27 and 28) are new in the TA literature. Much of the material on contract-making (Points 9–16) also appears for the first time in print in this book. This includes the *Outcome Matrix* model (Point 10); the distinction between an *action contract* and an *outcome contract* (Point 9); and the idea of a *finishable contract* (Point 12).

How this book relates to *TA Counselling in Action*

My book *Transactional Analysis Counselling in Action*, published by Sage in 1989, was also a practical guide to the use of TA in counselling and psychotherapy. In choosing the 30 suggestions for the present book, I have started from the principle that I would not duplicate the material in *TA Counselling in Action*. Instead, I have designed this book to be a complement to the earlier one, while still standing alone as a practical guide in its own right.

In *TA Counselling in Action*, I focused especially on the application of three TA models: the script matrix, the Discount Matrix, and the Racket System. I also added my own model of treatment planning.

In the present book, therefore, I have concentrated on other models. In particular, I have given thorough coverage to the Process Model, which I had to leave out of the earlier book for reasons of space. In the few instances where the material in the two books overlaps, this is because I say something in the present book that extends the practical usefulness of the topic concerned.

Thus this book and *TA Counselling in Action* stand alongside each other. My hope is that you will gain from reading the two books together. At the same time, you can read each book on its own without loss of usefulness.

---

1 A currently-available reference on the Process Model for non-clinicians is Taibi Kahler's book *The Mastery of Management*, published by Kahler Communications Inc., 1301 Scott Street, Little Rock, AR 72202, USA. Kahler's earlier booklets *Managing with the Process Communication Model* (1979a) and *Process Therapy in Brief* (1979b), and his book *Transactional Analysis Revisited* (1978) are now out of print.

'Counselling' and 'psychotherapy'

Different organisations have different ways of defining the distinction between 'counselling' and 'psychotherapy'. In this book I shall follow my usual practice, and treat the distinction as a matter for individual choice. The suggestions here apply to all ways of using TA to help personal change, whether that process be called 'counselling' or 'psychotherapy'. Throughout the book, I use the word 'counselling' in this extended sense.

When I use the term 'therapeutic', I mean it in its generic sense of 'curative'. This curative quality can be found either in counselling or in psychotherapy.

Pronouns, genders and names

I, Ian Stewart, am 'I'. You, the practitioner, are 'you'. Clients, and other people in general, are 'she' or 'he' at random. In the examples I use to illustrate the 30 suggestions, all clients' names are fictitious.

Thanks and acknowledgements

I wish first to acknowledge the generosity of Taibi Kahler. His *Process Model* provides the basis for an entire section in Part II of this book (Points 17–24). When I asked Taibi for permission to quote his work at length, he not only granted that permission, but sent me a detailed set of notes on his latest thinking.

Thanks also to my long-time colleague and fellow-director of The Berne Institute, Adrienne Lee. She and I have co-designed so many workshops and trainings that I find it difficult now to know which of the ideas in this book started in her mind and which in my own. I wish to thank her in particular for developing most of the material on the brief script questionnaire (Point 6).

I am grateful, too, for ideas and suggestions from the graduates and trainees of The Berne Institute. In particular, useful suggestions for this book have come from Diane Beechcroft, Steve Dennis and Maureen Lynch.

Every time I present training, do supervision, or run a workshop, I learn something new from my trainees, supervisees or audience. I thank all of them for what they have taught me. In this book, I hand some of their wisdom on to you.

Ian Stewart

I Principles of TA

An Outline of TA Theory

My aim in this first section is to give you a sketch of the theory of TA. I am assuming that you already have a working knowledge of TA ideas, and that you will use this introductory section simply as a brief aide-memoire. At the close of Part I, I shall list some sources for further reading on TA theory and practice.

Structure of TA theory

Eric Berne (1961, 1966, 1972) constructed TA theory in a sequence of four components, each of which builds on an understanding of the one before. They are:

- structural analysis (the ego-state model);
- analysis of transactions;
- game and racket analysis;
- script analysis.

In this sketch of TA theory, I shall begin with these four steps of Berne's sequence. Then I shall outline three further areas of theory that have been developed since Berne's death. They are:

- drivers and the Process Model;
- impasses and redecisions;
- discounting and redefining.

a. The ego-state model

Berne (1966: 364) defined an *ego-state* as 'a consistent pattern of feeling and experience directly related to a corresponding consistent pattern of behaviour'. Though Berne did not use the word 'thinking', it is clear from context that he meant thinking to be included as part of 'experience'.

In other words, an ego-state is a set of consistently related behaviours, thoughts and feelings. It is a way in which the person experiences herself and the world at any given moment, and in which she manifests that experience externally in her behaviour.

Berne's model comprises three distinct types of ego-state, known colloquially as *Parent, Adult* and *Child.*

At times, the person may behave, think and feel in ways which she 'borrowed' uncritically from one of her parents, or of others who were parent-figures for her. When she does so, she is said to be in a *Parent ego-state.*

Sometimes the person may regress to ways of behaving, thinking and feeling which he used when he was a child. Then he is said to be in a *Child ego-state.*

If the person is behaving, thinking and feeling in response to what is going on around him here and now, using all the resources available to him as a grown-up person, he is said to be in an *Adult ego-state.*

The initial capital letters – P, A, C – are a device to show that we are referring to the ego-states – Parent, Adult, Child. A small letter beginning the word shows we mean a real-life parent, adult or child.

Traditionally, the three types of ego-state are pictured in a diagram made up of three vertically-stacked circles, each labelled with its initial letter. Figure I.1 shows examples of this.

When we use the ego-state model to understand various aspects of personality, we are said to be employing *structural analysis.* The model is alternatively known as the *structural model.*

It is important to register that 'being in a Child ego-state' does *not* simply mean that the person is 'being childlike'. It means that she is replaying thoughts, feelings and behaviours that she first employed at a specific age in *her own childhood.*

Likewise, 'being in Parent' does *not* simply mean 'being parental'. It means that the person is using thinking, feelings and behaviours that she copied uncritically, as a child, from *her own* parents or parent-figures.

Second- and third-order structural analysis

In structural analysis, Parent or Child ego-states may sometimes be further subdivided. This is called *second-order* or *third-order* analysis, depending on the fineness of detail of the additional subdivisions.

In the case of Parent, second-order analysis involves distinguishing the various individual parent-figures that the person has introjected, and mapping the Parent, Adult and Child ego-states of each individual parent-figure.

For second-order analysis of Child, one of the person's Child

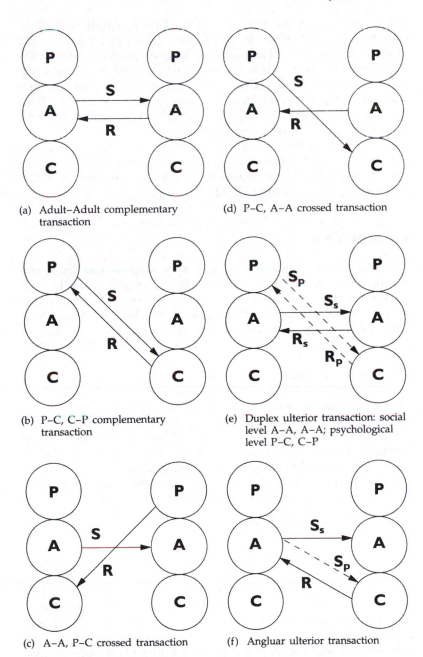

(a) Adult–Adult complementary transaction

(b) P–C, C–P complementary transaction

(c) A–A, P–C crossed transaction

(d) P–C, A–A crossed transaction

(e) Duplex ulterior transaction: social level A–A, A–A; psychological level P–C, C–P

(f) Angluar ulterior transaction

Figure I.1 *Types of transaction*

ego-states is analysed in terms of the Parent, Adult and Child ego-states that the person displayed when she was an actual child of the age in question. For example, suppose I regress to a 6-year-old Child ego-state. When I was an actual child of 6, I already had Parent, Adult and Child ego-states that were appropriate to a child of that age. Second-order analysis of my 6-year-old Child, then, maps out these age-appropriate ego-states, which I may still experience and express in adulthood.

Third-order analysis carries this process one stage further. For example, it might entail making an analysis of the still 'younger' Parent, Adult and Child ego-states that go to make up the Child ego-state in my 6-year-old Child.

b. Transactions

If I am communicating with you, I may address you from any one of my three types of ego-state: Parent, Adult or Child. The theory assumes also that I can 'aim' my communication for you to receive it in one of your Parent, Adult or Child ego-states. You have the same set of options in replying to me. This exchange of communications is known as a *transaction* (Berne 1966: 223–7; 1972: 20).

Examples of transactions are shown in Figure I.1. The arrows on the diagrams are known technically as *vectors*. They indicate the origin and the 'aim' of each communication.

In a *complementary transaction* (e.g. Figures I.1a and I.1b) the vectors are parallel and the ego-state addressed is the one which responds. Such communications have an easy, predictable feel to them, and the exchange may go on indefinitely.

A *crossed transaction* is one in which the vectors are not parallel, or in which the ego-state addressed is not the one which responds (e.g. Figures I.1c and I.1d). When a transaction is crossed, communication is interrupted and something different is likely to follow.

In an *ulterior transaction* (e.g. Figures I.1e and I.1f), two messages are being conveyed at the same time. The *social-level* message is what the communication is 'supposed to mean' on the surface. It is shown by the solid vectors. The *psychological-level* message is what the communication really means. It is indicated by the dotted ones.

Where the social-level and psychological-level messages contradict each other, there is said to be *incongruity* in the communication. In such cases, the behavioural outcome of the communication is determined at the psychological and not at the social level (Berne 1966: 227).

The use of the ego-state model to analyse sequences of transactions is often referred to as *transactional analysis proper*. The word 'proper' is added to show that we are talking about this branch of TA in particular, rather than TA as a whole.

Whenever I transact with another person, I signal recognition of her and she returns that recognition. In TA theory, any act of recognition is called a *stroke*. People need strokes to maintain their physical and psychological well-being. If the person is not receiving a satisfying number of *positive* (i.e. pleasant) strokes, he may unawarely revert to childhood strategies to gain *negative* (painful) strokes, following the principle: 'Any stroke is better than no stroke at all'.

c. Games and rackets

In childhood, the person may notice that in her family, certain feelings are encouraged while others are prohibited. To get her strokes, she may decide to feel only the permitted feelings. This decision is made without conscious awareness. As a grown-up, she may at times continue to cover her authentic feelings with the feelings that were permitted to her in her childhood. These substitute feelings are known in TA as *racket feelings* (English 1971, 1972).

TA assumes that authentic emotions are four in number. In traditional colloquial language, these are 'mad, sad, scared and glad'. ('Mad', here, is used in its American sense of 'angry'.) These four emotions, however, are not always authentic. It is possible also to feel racket anger, sadness, scare or happiness.

The person may employ stereotyped sequences of behaviour to 'justify' experiencing racket feelings (e.g. habitually 'losing' a car key and feeling anxious). Such behaviour patterns are called *rackets*.

A *game* is a repetitive sequence of transactions in which both parties end up experiencing racket feelings. It always includes a *switch*, a moment when both players suddenly change roles (Berne 1972). People play games without being aware they are doing so.

d. Script

Eric Berne (1972) suggested that every person, in childhood, writes a life-story for himself. This story has a beginning, a middle and an end. The person writes the basic plot in his infant years, before he is old enough to talk more than a few words. Later on in childhood, he will typically add more detail to the story, and the main plot is likely to have been laid down by the age of 7. The incidental details of the story may be revised or elaborated during adolescence.

In grown-up life, the person is usually no longer consciously aware of the life-story he has written for himself. Yet, especially at times of stress, he may often act it out. Without being aware of it, he may set up successive episodes in his life so that he moves towards the final scene he decided upon as an infant. This preconscious life-story is known in TA as the *life-script* or simply the *script*.

The concept of script ranks with the ego-state model as a central building-block of TA. *Script analysis* means the use of various procedures to help uncover the preconscious material that makes up the person's script.

Berne (1972: 84) suggested that the script is predicated on one of four *positions*. These are deeply-ingrained convictions about the worth of self and others, which the child adopts at an early stage of development. The four positions (often known today as 'life positions') are:

- I'm OK, you're OK;
- I'm OK, you're not-OK;
- I'm not-OK, you're OK;
- I'm not-OK, you're not-OK.

The *script matrix* (Steiner 1966, 1974) is a model that shows how parents may pass *script messages* to the child. A blank script matrix is shown in Figure I.2. The messages passed down from the Parent in the parent to the Parent in the child are known as *counterinjunctions*. These typically comprise 'oughts and shoulds', parental value-judgements, and verbal commands about what the child should or should not be or do. Counterinjunctions are messages that the child receives in later childhood, when she has developed a good command of language.

Script messages passed from the Adult in the parent, and housed in the Adult of the child, are called *program messages*, and typically begin 'Here's how to . . .'.

Messages passed from the Child of the parent, and received in the Child of the child, are called *injunctions* if they are negative and restrictive (e.g. Don't Exist, Don't Be You), and *permissions* if they give the child positive choices (e.g. It's OK to Exist, It's OK to Be You). These Child messages are typically received by the

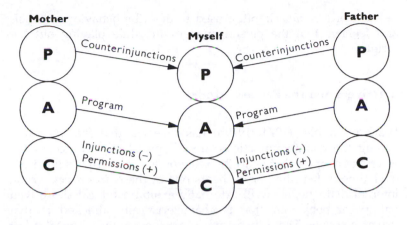

Figure I.2   *The script matrix* (*Source*: Stewart and Joines 1987: 129)

child during earlier childhood, before she has full command of language. They are initially transmitted non-verbally by the parent, though they may be reinforced verbally later. Injunctions find their origins in unmet Child needs in the parent, and are usually passed on to the child without the parent's awareness.

Mary and Robert Goulding (1979: 34–9) have listed 12 injunctions that turn up time and again in script analysis. They are:

- Don't Exist
- Don't Be You (sometimes, Don't Be the Sex You Are)
- Don't Be a Child (or, Don't Enjoy)
- Don't Grow Up (or, Don't Leave Me)
- Don't Make It (Don't Succeed)
- Don't (i.e. Don't Do Anything)
- Don't Be Important
- Don't Belong
- Don't Be Close
- Don't Be Well (or, Don't Be Sane)
- Don't Think
- Don't Feel.

The parents' messages cannot *make* the child develop a particular script, though they can exert a powerful influence upon it. In the last analysis, the child *decides* which of the messages to follow. These *early decisions* are arrived at with a young child's powers of reasoning and reality-testing.

The word *'scripty'* is often used to describe behaviours, beliefs and feelings that the person engages in while playing out her script.

e. Drivers and the Process Model

Work by Kahler (1974, 1979b) has revealed that five messages among the counterinjunctions are of special significance to the *process* of script – that is, to the issue of *how* the script is lived out over time. When the person hears one of these *driver messages* in internal dialogue, she will externally exhibit a typical short-lived pattern of behaviour that is characteristically attached to that driver message. These 'behaviour packages', which typically last for about half a second at a time, are known as *driver behaviours*.

Following TA tradition, Kahler used colloquial language to label the five drivers. He called them *Be Perfect, Be Strong, Try Hard, Please You* and *Hurry Up.*

Driver behaviours are not specific to any culture, language, age group, educational background, or other feature of personality. There is some evidence that persons from different cultures may show the five driver behaviours with differing relative intensities, but everyone shows all five drivers from time to time. No other driver behaviours but these five have yet been discovered.

Driver behaviours are significant for several reasons. First, they appear to be a 'gateway into script'. Immediately before a person engages in scripty behaviour or experiences a racket feeling, she will always show one of the driver behaviours. The drivers themselves are external indicators that the person is replaying a specific script belief internally. I shall say more about the applications of this in Point 17.

Second, observation of drivers is the key to quick and reliable diagnosis of many other aspects of the script. It is the basis of the diagnostic system known as the *Process Model* (Kahler 1979b; Ware 1983). I shall describe this in detail in the third section of Part II (Points 17–24).

Script process

The detailed *content* of each person's script is unique to that person, though various broad categories of script message can be distinguished (see the section on 'Script' above). By contrast, script *process* seems to fall into a relatively small number of distinctive patterns (numbered at six or seven, depending on the TA writer quoted). For reasons that are not fully understood, these patterns also appear to be uniform across cultural boundaries.

A person's process script type is closely correlated with her driver behaviours. I shall discuss process scripts, and their link with drivers, more fully in Point 20.

f. Impasses and redecisions

The *redecision school* of TA combines the theoretical framework of TA with concepts and techniques from Gestalt therapy (Goulding and Goulding 1978, 1979). A central notion of the redecision approach is that of the *impasse* – a 'stuck place' in which the person experiences two conflicting urges, but does not act on either, and uses a lot of energy in remaining stuck.

Fritz Perls, the founder of Gestalt therapy, had characterised the impasse as an internal struggle between 'topdog and under-dog' (Perls 1971). Robert and Mary Goulding framed Perls' ideas in TA terms by suggesting that the intrapsychic struggle was being fought out between two different ego-states. Thus, the person might experience a conflict between an internal Parental voice urging him to 'Work hard!' and his Child response of 'Don't want to!'.

In the Gouldings' model of personal change, the *decisional* nature of script is stressed. It is assumed that, because it was the child who made the original script decision, it will be in the Child ego-state that the person can most powerfully change that decision in the here-and-now. Such a new decision in Child is called a *redecision*.

g. Redefining and discounting

The young child decides on a life-script because it represents the best strategy that the child can work out to survive and get his needs met in what often seems a hostile world. When the person is in a Child ego-state, he may still be believing that any threat to his infant picture of the world is a threat to the satisfaction of his needs, or even to his survival. Thus he may sometimes distort his perception of reality so that it fits his script. When the person does this, he is said to be *redefining* (Mellor and Sigmund 1975b).

The sum total of the person's perception of the world at any given moment – including both those aspects which he is redefining and those which he is not – is called the *frame of reference* (Schiff et al. 1975).

One way in which the person can ensure that the world seems to fit her script is to selectively ignore information available to her about a situation. Without conscious intention, she blanks out the aspects of the situation that would contradict her script. This is called *discounting* (Mellor and Sigmund 1975a).

As a part of maintaining their scripts, people may sometimes get into relationships as grown-ups which replay the relationships they had with their parents when they were children. This is done without conscious awareness. In this situation, one of the partners in the relationship may play the part of Parent and Adult, while the other acts Child. Between them, the two people then function as though they had only three instead of six classes of ego-state available. Thus both parties are discounting some of their ego-state options. A relationship like this is called a *symbiosis* (Schiff et al. 1975).

These ideas form the basis for the theory and practice of the *Cathexis* (or *Schiffian*) school of current TA.

Principles of TA Treatment

h. Treatment philosophy

The philosophy of TA treatment rests upon three assumptions. These are as follows:

- People are OK;
- Everyone has the capacity to think;
- People decide their own destiny, and these decisions can be changed.

From these assumptions there follow two basic principles of TA practice:

- contractual method;
- open communication.

Contractual method plays such an important part in TA practice that I give it its own separate sub-section below.

People are OK

This means: everyone has intrinsic worth, value and dignity. This is a statement of essence rather than behaviour, and is held to be true irrespective of race, age, gender, religion, or any other personal feature.

Everyone has the capacity to think

Everyone except the severely brain-damaged has the capacity to think. Therefore it is the responsibility of each of us to decide what he or she wants from life. Each individual will ultimately live with the consequences of what he or she decides.

Decisional model

TA holds that when the person engages in script behaviours, she is following strategies she *decided* upon as a young child. The child was not *made* to feel or behave in particular ways by her parents, or by 'the environment'. TA assumes that the same is true for the adult person. Other people, or our life circumstances, may exert strong pressures on him, but it is always his own decision whether to conform to these pressures. The person is thus held to be personally *responsible* for all his feelings and behaviour.

Since the person is responsible for taking script decisions, it follows that he can later change any of these decisions. If some of his infant decisions are producing uncomfortable results for him in adult life, he can trace the dysfunctional decisions and change them for new and more appropriate ones.

Thus, TA takes an assertive view of the possibility of personal change. The person will achieve change not merely by gaining 'insight' into old patterns of behaviour, but by deciding to change those patterns and taking action to achieve this change.

Open communication

Eric Berne insisted that the client, as well as the practitioner, should have full information about what was going on in their work together. This follows from the basic assumptions that people are OK and that everyone can think.

In TA practice, case notes are open to the client's inspection. The practitioner may often encourage the client to learn the ideas of TA. These measures invite the client to take an equal role with the counsellor in the process of change.

i. Contractual method

The TA practitioner assumes that he and his client will take *joint responsibility* for achieving whatever change the client wants to make. This follows from the assumption that counsellor and client relate on equal terms. It is not the counsellor's task to do things *to* the client. Nor can the client expect that the counsellor will do everything *for* him.

Since both parties take an equal share in the process of change, it is important that both know clearly how the task will be shared. Therefore they enter into a *contract*. Eric Berne defined this as: 'an explicit bilateral commitment to a well-defined course of action' (Berne 1966: 362).

Claude Steiner (1974) has suggested four requirements for sound contract-making. These are widely accepted by transactional analysts. They are:

1   *Mutual consent*: counsellor and client must explicitly agree the terms of the contract.
2   *Valid consideration*: the client must give the counsellor some agreed recompense for the service that the counsellor offers. This will usually be financial, but other forms of consideration are also possible.
3   *Competency*: the counsellor must have skills to provide the service contracted for. The client must also be competent to undertake counselling; for example, she must have sufficient Adult ego-state available to understand and agree to what is going on in the session.
4   *Lawful object*: everything agreed on in the contract must be legal, and must meet appropriate professional and ethical norms.

The term *overall contract* is used to describe the client's main longer-term contract. This will often be for an important script change. Client and counsellor are likely to address the overall contract over a number of sessions or for the full duration of counselling. A *session contract*, as its name implies, is a shorter-term contract taken for a single session, or even for part of the time within one session. A *(working) assignment* means a contract for some activity that the client will carry out between one session and the next.

In the second section of Part II, I shall discuss the technique of contract-making in detail (Points 9–16).

j. Treatment direction

TA is an actionistic approach to personal change. The TA practitioner does not assume that the 'counselling relationship', of itself, will necessarily bring about desired changes. Instead, she develops an analysis of the client's problem, and agrees a contract for the changes he will make. She then intervenes actively in a planned and structured manner to help him achieve these changes. This process of planned intervention is summed up in the phrase *treatment direction*.

I have defined treatment direction as 'the informed choice of interventions to facilitate the client in achieving the agreed contract, in the light of [the counsellor's] diagnosis of the client' (Stewart 1989: 9).

There is a continual three-way interplay between contract, diagnosis and treatment direction. For example, you may revise your diagnosis of the client because you have got to know her better or because she has already changed in the course of treatment. The changed diagnosis may call for a renegotiation of the contract; and the new diagnosis and new contract will then require you to rethink your choice of interventions. Figure I.3, which I call the 'Treatment Triangle', pictures this continuous three-way interaction.

k. The 'three Ps': permission, protection and potency

Crossman (1966) suggested that a crucial function of the therapist was to give the client *permission* to go against the prejudicial commands of the Parent 'in her head'. To do this, said Crossman, the therapist had to convince the client that she had more *potency* – more power – than that internal Parent. At the same time, the therapist needed to provide the client with appropriate *protection* from the wrath of the internal Parent, at least until the client could develop his own protection. This trilogy – of permission, protection and potency – is now usually referred to in TA simply as the 'three Ps'.

Practitioners in the redecision school of TA play down the significance of 'permission-giving' in Crossman's sense. Instead, they see the client herself as *taking permission* to go against the script. They argue that it is the client, not the therapist, who possesses the potency to make this change.

Transactional analysts from all schools, however, would agree on the central importance of ensuring protection for the client. In practical terms, this includes setting up a physically safe environment, guaranteeing confidentiality, and using an effective system for medical and psychiatric referral. Another crucial element of protection is to guard against the three tragic script outcomes: suicide, homicide or going crazy. This is accomplished by inviting the client to 'close escape hatches' – that is, to renounce these three outcomes permanently and unconditionally (see below and Point 7).

l. Closing escape hatches

A distinctive feature of TA treatment is the procedure known as *closing escape hatches* (Drye et al. 1973; Holloway 1973; Boyd and Cowles-Boyd 1980; Stewart 1989: 81–92). To close escape hatches,

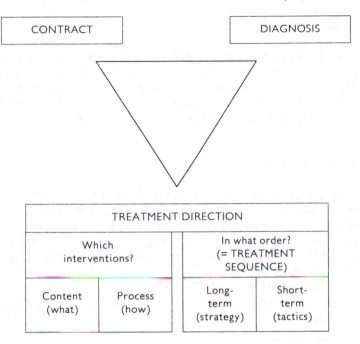

CONTRACT		DIAGNOSIS	

TREATMENT DIRECTION			
Which interventions?		In what order? (= TREATMENT SEQUENCE)	
Content (what)	Process (how)	Long-term (strategy)	Short-term (tactics)

Figure I.3   *The Treatment Triangle* (*Source*: Guichard 1987, with modifications by present author)

the client makes and states an unconditional decision that she will never, in any circumstances, kill or harm self, kill or harm anyone else, or go crazy. This undertaking is not a *promise* to the counsellor; it is a decision that the client takes for herself. The counsellor's task is to offer the procedure, then act as witness while feeding back to the client any sign of incongruity.

The closing of escape hatches has two purposes. First, it serves as practical protection against the tragic outcomes of suicide, homicide or going crazy. Second, it facilitates movement out of script. Experience of script analysis indicates that many people's scripts are directed towards a final scene (*script payoff*) that entails one of the three tragic outcomes. The form of the child's early decision in such cases is: 'If things get bad enough, I can always . . . (kill myself, kill someone else, go crazy)'. By closing escape hatches, the person takes an unconditional Adult decision to turn away from these outcomes. The intrapsychic effect of this is to destabilise the entire structure of the script, making therapeutic movement easier. This therapeutic shift may sometimes be bought at the cost of some temporary discomfort to the client.

m. Confrontation

It is an axiom of TA method that the task of the counsellor is to *confront* the client's script. The term 'confrontation', here, does not imply the use of aggressive or harsh interventions. It means, simply, *any* move that the counsellor makes to invite the client to test her script beliefs against here-and-now reality.

n. Concepts of 'cure'

Eric Berne urged that the proper goal of TA treatment is not 'insight', nor 'progress', but *cure*. While most of today's transactional analysts agree with Berne that cure is their goal, they have differing views about what constitutes cure. Some simply equate cure with completion of the treatment contract between client and counsellor.

Berne himself (1961: 160–75; 1972: 362–4) saw cure not as a once-off event, but as a progressive process that moved through four stages:

- social control;
- symptomatic relief;
- transference cure;
- script cure.

At the first stage, *social control*, the client may still feel the discomforts and troubles she has brought to counselling, but she has become able to control dysfunctional behaviours in her interactions with others. Moving to *symptomatic relief*, the client now also experiences relief of subjective discomforts such as anxiety, depression or confusion. In *transference cure*, the person has become able to stay out of script so long as he can 'keep the therapist around', either literally or in his head. Finally, at the stage of *script cure*, the person's own Adult takes over the intrapsychic role of the therapist, making it possible for the person to 'put a new show on the road'. This means that she moves substantially and permanently out of script patterns and into script-free thinking, feeling and behaviour.

Transactional analysts who favour the redecision approach (see above) are more likely to speak of redecision as the final stage of cure. They would also demote the importance of 'transference cure', since the redecision practitioner's objective is to shift transference away from herself throughout treatment (Goulding and Goulding 1979: 49).

Autonomy

As another way of framing 'cure', Eric Berne proposed the idea that the goal of personal change is *autonomy*. He did not give a definition for autonomy, but suggested that it would be manifested by 'the release or recovery of three capacities: awareness, spontaneity and intimacy' (Berne 1964: 158–60). *Awareness*, in Berne's terms, means the ability to experience the world directly, without interpretation or preconceptions. *Spontaneity* means the ability to exercise one's full options in moving between ego-states. By *intimacy*, Berne meant the free, uncensored expression of feelings and wants, without games or manipulation.

Recommended further reading

Eric Berne's original writings are essential reading for anyone using TA in therapeutic settings. I recommend three of his books in particular:

> *Transactional Analysis in Psychotherapy* (Berne 1961);
> *Principles of Group Treatment* (Berne 1966); and
> *What Do You Say After You Say Hello?* (Berne 1972).

The best-selling *Games People Play* (Berne 1964), though an amusing 'read', is not a clear statement of Berne's theories.

You will find a full account of the basic theory of modern TA in *TA Today* (Stewart and Joines 1987). My book *Transactional Analysis Counselling in Action* (Stewart 1989) contains practical guidance on the application of TA to counselling and psychotherapy.

Two books by Robert and Mary Goulding are highly recommended reading on the 'redecision' approach in TA. They are *Changing Lives Through Redecision Therapy* (Goulding and Goulding 1979) and *The Power is in the Patient* (Goulding and Goulding 1978).

You will find the main principles of the 'Cathexis' (Schiffian) approach in *The Cathexis Reader* (Schiff et al. 1975).

If you would like a historical perspective on Eric Berne and the system of TA that he developed, you can turn to my book on *Eric Berne* in Sage Publications' series *Key Figures in Counselling and Psychotherapy* (Stewart 1992).

II   Thirty Ways to Develop your TA Counselling

First Principles

There are two reasons why I have called this section 'First principles'. The topics it covers are all central to effective practice in TA. They are all, also, things to think about early in the process of counselling.

The first four Points in the section are about attitudes and ways of thinking, rather than techniques. I know this book's main purpose is to offer you *practical* recommendations to help you develop your counselling. But to my mind, acquiring an attitude is just as 'practical' as learning a technique, and just as useful.

In fact, you could argue that acquiring an attitude is the more practical. When you learn a technique, you get just that one technique, no less, no more. When you have acquired an attitude, you can use it to generate many techniques.

1   Presuppose the 'one-session cure'

Eric Berne used to urge his students to 'cure their patients in one session'. In this first Point, I am suggesting that you open your mind to this ideal of Berne's, the 'one-session cure'.

Some traditionally-minded professionals might find Berne's recommendation startling, to say the least. They might feel that it trivialises the long and tortuous process which (for them) marks out the true course of personal change. Indeed, some transactional analysts have sought to make Berne look more 'respectable' by pointing out that this was just one example of his trick of making valid points through the use of exaggeration. Everybody knows, they say, that it is usually not possible to cure people in a single session; Berne was just finding a striking way of pointing out that the counsellor needs to be proactive in her approach to treatment.

Indeed, this was part of what Berne was doing. But I think he was doing more. In his demand that we 'cure our patients in one session', he was *presupposing* two other statements:

1   People can be cured;
2   Cure can be quick.

My first counsel to you, then, is to keep your mind open to these two presuppositions of Berne's. As you begin working with each client, do so on the assumption that people can be cured. Assume, too, that they can be cured quickly.

This is not the same as old-fashioned 'positive thinking'. It is a way of framing what you know, or think you know, about how you can help people to change.

Why is this presupposition valuable?

If you start each case by presupposing that people *can* be cured quickly, two outcomes are then possible: either your client *will* be cured quickly, or she will not.

If, on the other hand, you begin the case by presupposing that people *cannot* be cured quickly, then it is certain that your client *will not* be cured quickly. One obvious practical reason for this is that you will not have been aiming for speedy cure anyway. Why should you, a responsible professional, aim for something that you are presupposing to be impossible? Indeed, even if your client were to get better quickly, then you would have to judge this a purely chance event, since you have presupposed that your treatment could not have been the cause.

In other words: you and your clients have everything to gain, and nothing to lose, if you choose to presuppose that quick cure is possible.

Presuppositions do not pre-empt facts

In inviting you to 'presuppose one-session cure', I am not suggesting that you should use presuppositions as a substitute for proper diagnosis and systematic treatment planning. On the contrary, as I stress in several of the coming Points, these factual procedures are essential to your effectiveness.

Presuppositions are not about such factual issues; they are sweeping, generalised beliefs about 'what *can* be true, what *cannot* be true, what *must* or *must not* happen'. Presuppositions are usually not subjected to factual investigation, because they are held to be non-controversial. Indeed, factual investigation begins where presuppositions leave off.[1]

Open v. closed presuppositions

Eric Berne chose his two presuppositions, 'People can be cured, and they can be cured quickly', because he wanted to counter two opposing presuppositions that he often heard put forth by the psychoanalytic establishment of his time. They were:

1 'People are never cured through counselling or psycho-therapy; at most, you can expect them to "make progress" or "gain insight".'
2 'Effective treatment must take a long time.'

You will notice that both these statements are absolutes. They presuppose that 'cure *never* happens,' and that effective treatment *'must* be slow'. Thus, both these statements close off possibilities. I call such statements *closed presuppositions*.

By contrast, Berne's presuppositions talk of 'what may happen'. He does not suggest that people are always cured by coming to counselling, but that they can be cured. Likewise, he does not assume that cure must always be achieved quickly, but rather that it can be. Both statements open up possibilities. Thus I call them *open presuppositions*.

A few more presuppositions

To conclude this Point, I shall copy Berne's habit of throwing out thought-provoking ideas with little comment, and list another four closed presuppositions. I have heard all these being put forth by the counselling and therapeutic 'establishment' of *our* time (in TA as well as elsewhere). In each case I shall suggest an open presupposition to put alongside the closed one.

My purpose is not to prove that the closed presupposition is necessarily 'wrong', nor to argue that the open presupposition is always 'right'. Like Berne, I am simply inviting you to examine each presupposition, and be aware how far it has been an influence on your own practice as a counsellor or psychotherapist.

---

1 A full account of the nature and logic of presuppositions would take me far beyond my practical brief in this book. For a fascinating discussion, see O'Hanlon and Wilk 1987.

1(a) *Closed presupposition*: To be effective, counselling *must* deal with the person's past.
1(b) *Open presupposition*: Effective counselling *can* focus mainly on the present and the future.

2(a) *Closed presupposition*: To work effectively as a counsellor, you *must* 'be yourself'.
2(b) *Open presupposition*: When you work as a counsellor, you have a choice between many different 'selves', all of which are authentic. You *can* choose which 'self' to be, from session to session and from moment to moment, in a way that best meets the needs of your client.

3(a) *Closed presupposition*: Effective counselling *must* rest wholly in the relationship between counsellor and client.
3(b) *Open presupposition*: Effective counselling *can* be accomplished through technique as well as through the relationship.

4(a) *Closed presupposition*: Profound personal change in counselling *must* be painful, as the person faces up to distress and discomfort held from her childhood.
4(b) *Open presupposition*: Profound personal change *can* be comfortable, easy and fun. The person *can* simply choose to let go of childhood pain and discomforts, leaving them where they belong: in the past.

Self-supervision: presuppositions about personal change

1   Take a large piece of paper and write at the top: 'Effective counselling *must* . . .'. Then write down all the ways you can think of to finish the sentence. If you are working in a group, you may choose to 'brainstorm' sentence completions.

2   Next, go through each of the completed sentences. For each sentence, now write another sentence that begins 'Effective counselling *can* . . .' and which ends by saying the *opposite* to your original sentence. For example, if you had first written 'Effective counselling *must* take place within a close relationship', you would now write something like: 'Effective counselling *can* take place without any close relationship.'

3   For each of these 'opposite' statements, make out a case why that statement might be true. For example, could it be that counselling *without* a close relationship might avoid some of the pitfalls of transference?

4 Finally, go through the pairs of statements, and consider for each pair: rather than 'either-or', could the situation better be described with 'both-and'? For example, could it be that effective counselling demands a close relationship with some clients, but a distant relationship with others?

Key point

Be aware of your presuppositions about personal change.

Keep them under review, and be ready to open out any that you find to be rigid or limiting.

---

2 Stay aware of time-frames

The three time-frames are: *past, present* and *future.* In this Point, I recommend that as you work with TA, it pays to stay aware of these three time-frames. I shall suggest how you can use them and how they can constrain you.

Time-frames and TA

The time dimension is a central organising principle in TA theory. It is at the heart of the ego-state model itself. Parent and Child ego-states are both echoes of the *past*: Parent represents ego-states borrowed in the person's own past from her actual parents or parent-figures, while Child denotes ego-states replayed from the person's own past, that is, her childhood. Only in the Adult ego-state is the person responding to the *present* with her full present resources.

The ego-state model has no place for the future time-frame. However, the central TA principle of *treatment direction* represents a way to work with the future. In the light of the person's *past* history, her *present* wants and resources are directed contractually towards a clearly-defined *future* outcome that she desires.

The upside-down tree

When I am running TA psychotherapy or training sessions, I often put up on the wall a poster that I have designed. It is shown in miniature in Figure 2.1. As you will see, it pictures a tree upside down. Among the roots of the tree, at the top of the picture, are the words: 'Your roots are in the future'.

Half-way up the trunk of the tree (so half-way down the picture) are the words: 'Action is in the present'.

Among the branches at the top of the tree (thus, at the bottom of the picture), the poster says: 'The past is for information only'.

Why is the tree upside down? For two reasons. First: as a picture of personal change, it turns many traditional attitudes on their heads. Second: it portrays a process of change in which the client dynamically pulls herself upwards towards a future outcome, rather than looking downwards at a muddy bog of past problems from which she must struggle to free herself. It is this process of 'pulling upwards' that is represented by the three slogans on the tree, ranged upwards from past to future.

There is a way in which all three of the phrases on the poster are self-evident in their meaning. However, I think it is worth while to underline some of their implications for the process of change in counselling.

'Your roots are in the future'

Many traditional approaches to personal change have stressed the importance of analysing the person's past experience. The past, on this traditional view, is the 'soil' from which the person grows – where she 'finds her roots'.

Yet in reality, if someone decides she wants to make personal changes now, she cannot find these changes in the past. The past is finished and unchangeable. Nor can past experience itself ever be an absolute barrier to future change (unless the past experience has resulted in physical impairment). In this light, the idea that we 'have our roots in the past' turns out to be a limiting illusion.

To find her changes, the person must instead look to the future: to the positive outcomes that she desires. Having chosen these future outcomes, she can begin to pull herself towards them.

It is in that sense that our roots are in the future. In the future also, we may find many fascinating and useful routes.

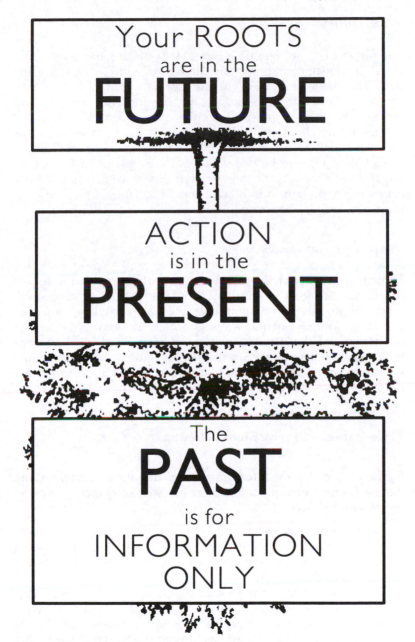

Figure 2.1 *The upside-down tree*

'Action is in the present'

The present is a strange time-frame. It is always here, yet never here. If we imagine it, it is really the future; if we recall it, it is the past. Eric Berne (1961: 37) cut the Gordian knot of this conundrum by following the lead of his mentor Paul Federn, and defined 'the present' arbitrarily as the current period of 24 hours.

Whether we choose to define the present as a split second or as a day, it is only in the present that we can actually *do* anything. If I want the future to be different from the past, then I must do something in the present to bring that difference about. If I am a counsellor and want to facilitate people to change, I must also do my facilitating in the present.

'The past is for information only'

Though we cannot change the past, it would be foolish to ignore it, in counselling or in life generally. The past is a huge storehouse of useful information. In particular, analysing our past allows us to pick out the ways in which we may have limited ourselves, and the ways in which we have acted most successfully to gain outcomes we wanted. In the light of this information, we can make effective choices about what strategies to use in the present to move to desired outcomes in the future.

Time-frames and treatment planning

Figure 2.2 pictures the three time-frames in a more formal setting: that of TA treatment planning. Here are some comments on what the diagram shows.

1 *History-taking*, by definition, relates to the *past*.
2 *Script analysis* is a *link between past and present*. It is a way in which past information about the client can be systematically related to the present.
3 *Diagnosis* relates to the *present*. In TA usage, 'diagnosis' does not mean a once-and-for-all label that is permanently attached to the client. It is, rather, a process of assessment that is constantly being reviewed and updated. As the ever-moving present travels through time, your diagnosis of your client is likely to change. This may be because you have come to know more about him in the course of your work together, and/or

'Effective counselling is
OUTCOME-POWERED'

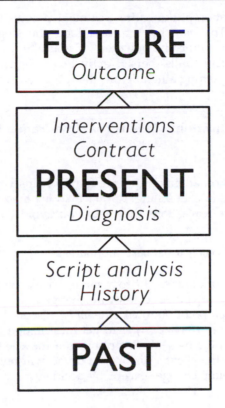

Figure 2.2 *Time-frames and treatment planning*

because he has made personal changes during counselling that lead you to alter your diagnostic assessment.

4 *Contract-making* is also carried out in the present, and serves to *link the present to the future.* As the present moves on in time, your client and you may agree many changes in the active contract. Some of these will be because the client has achieved, changed or abandoned goals. Others will relate to your ever-changing diagnosis. (Recall the 'Treatment Triangle', Part I.j.)

5 The *outcome* of counselling always stays in the future. Why? Because as soon as a desired outcome is achieved – that is,

arrives in the present – it is no longer an aim of counselling. At any such point of achievement, the client and counsellor may decide together to move to termination; or they may agree to begin work on another of the client's desired outcomes.

6   The orientation of the entire treatment process is towards the outcome. That is why I have added the slogan: 'Effective counselling is outcome-powered'. If you like, you can imagine that the client 'pulls' herself actively through the process of change by 'getting a handle on' the future outcome she wants.

Practical applications of the three time-frames in treatment

In my experience, attention to time-frames helps you avoid some common errors in counselling. Rather than list these errors, I shall list the positive realisations that help you avoid the errors.

Use history-taking only to get past information

As Figure 2.2 underlines, history-taking deals with the client's past. That past, of course, cannot be changed.

One practical point follows: the *only* reason for looking at someone's history (their past) is to get information that may help them change in the present. Tempting as it may be to spend time 'talking about' the client's history, to do so will not in itself lead to any therapeutic change, except by accident.

Script analysis is a present road-map of the past

Script analysis, too, tells us how the person decided to be in the past. It does not necessarily describe how they are in the present. Its use is as a *present* road-map of the *past* that will assist change in the *future*.

Arising from this is the practical recommendation: when you are doing script analysis, make it explicit to your client that what you are investigating is how they decided to be in the past. Make it clear too that this past map does not bind them in the present or future. On the contrary, it lets them see more clearly what they may now need to change in the present to get what they want in the future.

Keep your present diagnosis under review

Because the present is ever-changing, the client's diagnosis also may well change as counselling goes on. If the process of counselling seems to have 'got stuck', one feature to check is whether your diagnosis of the client has itself 'got stuck' – that is, has failed to change as the client has changed.

'Early-scene work' is in the present, not the past

It is especially important to bear time-frames in mind when you are doing any form of 'early-scene work'. This is work in which you ask the client to 'go back to the past' in imagination and 'redo' a past scene (Goulding and Goulding 1979: 190–4; Stewart 1989: 144–5).

For the practical success of techniques like this, you need to invite the client to '*be* in the past scene', re-experiencing it fully as if she were really there. Indeed, you need to join the client in the 'reality' of this imagined experience.

Yet, at the same time, you as facilitator need to be keenly aware that in reality you are *not* 'working in the past'. That would be impossible. What you are doing, instead, is working in the present with the client's recalled experience of the past.

Crucially then, to achieve change in work of this kind, you need to facilitate the client to bring her *present resources* into that recalled past experience. With the aid of these present resources, she can then make the recalled scene work out in a new way. Her final step is to realise that in any similar scenes in the *future*, she can use these present resources to achieve an outcome that is different from the old scripty one.

This is the rationale behind the Gouldings' warning that in early-scene work, 'The others are not to be changed' (Goulding and Goulding 1979: 206; Stewart 1989: 143). In redoing the re-called past scene, you should never have the client imagine someone else in the scene taking the initiative that makes the difference. Instead, it must always be the client's recalled self who makes the move to bring about the changed outcome.

Look to the outcome, not the problem

People often come to counselling to 'solve a problem'. However, in the context of the three time-frames, it is more constructive to regard the person's problem as belonging to the *past*. This helps us see that the task of counselling is to help the person use his *present* resources to achieve a desired *future* outcome.

TA trainer Ken Mellor (workshop presentation) puts it well when he advises: 'Look forward to the outcome, not backward at the problem.'

Contracts are different from outcomes

Figure 2.2 confirms that when you work out a contract for change, the contract is a *present means* of achieving a desired *future outcome*. The contract, then, is not the same thing as the outcome. I shall say more about this in the section below on 'Contract-making'.

Key point

Be aware of the three time-frames: *past*, *present* and *future*. Know what you can and cannot do in each time-frame.

   Consider the slogan: 'Effective counselling is outcome-powered'. Look forward to the outcome, not backward to the problem.

---

3   Line up the row of dominoes

Richard Bandler (1985: 111) suggests that doing effective therapy is like lining up a row of dominoes. It may take you a long while, says Bandler, to take the dominoes out of their box and painstakingly, one after another, set them up in line. But then – just one flick of your finger to the last domino in the line, and down go the whole lot.

I recommend Bandler's approach to you in this Point. As you work with your client, I suggest that you take as much time and as much care as is necessary to get that line of dominoes set up just as you want it. Then, when the time comes, one gentle flick of your therapeutic finger may be all that is needed for your client to collapse his problems like a line of tumbling dominoes.

TA offers us a particularly well-defined 'line of dominoes' to set up. The key TA concept here is that of *treatment sequence*. This is the process by which successive stages of treatment are carried out in a specific order.

Nine steps into script change

Here are nine 'dominoes' that TA practice recommends you to line up, starting from the point when you have made initial contact with your client. They are all steps to complete *before* beginning your specific interventions to invite script change. They are as follows:

1 Carry out *intake* and make *initial diagnosis.*
2 Consider *referral.*
3 Set *ground rules.*
4 Negotiate the *business contract.*
5 Ask the client to complete a *goals list.*
6 Make a more complete diagnosis, which may include *script analysis.*
7 Agree the initial *treatment contract.*
8 Develop a *treatment plan,* including sessional contracts.
9 Facilitate the client to *close escape hatches.*

Avoid rushing into 'the work'

In my experience, the tempting error is to rush ahead into 'the work' *before* you get this pack of nine dominoes properly lined up. There is seductive attraction in the idea of 'getting straight to the point', especially if 'the point' promises to entail some kind of dramatic feeling release for the client. But if you do this before you have a clear contract, or before you have a well-formed idea of the client's diagnosis, then you have left a gap in the dominoes. When the time comes to flick the end one, you may find that you have simply knocked that one flat and left the rest standing.

The order of the nine steps

The detailed order of these nine steps is open to some variation. For example, some practitioners prefer to present their ground rules to potential clients before even carrying out an intake interview. Also, some stages may be merged: many transactional analysts would consider the setting of rules to be an integral part of negotiating the business contract.

However, some features of the order cannot be violated without disrupting the effectiveness of the treatment sequence. Here are four rules that are, for practical purposes, unbreakable:

1   You must check and clear the possible need for *psychiatric or medical referral* before you can go on to any of the later stages.
2   You must set your *ground rules* and negotiate the *business contract* before you negotiate the treatment contract.
3   You must make an initial *diagnosis* of the client before you can work out an appropriate treatment contract.
4   You must ensure that the client has congruently *closed escape hatches* before you invite her to engage in any behaviour that would entail her moving out of script.

Time-scale

These nine steps apply not only to the whole time-scale of your treatment plan, but also over shorter spans of time. You can apply them also to:

● subsections of the treatment plan;
● individual counselling sessions;
● each intervention within the session.

On these shorter time-scales, it may not be necessary or possible to repeat all the nine steps. However, I suggest it is always a good idea to keep them in mind and review them. Here are some ways in which this applies.

Sub-sections of the treatment plan

Typically in the course of treatment, the process of change is divided into various subsections over time. It is usual for the client to 'recycle' personal issues as treatment goes on (Erskine 1973; Stewart 1989: 9–14). Each time a particular issue arises, this may be taken as beginning a particular subsection of the treatment plan. Again, the client will be likely to make and fulfil various different contracts as treatment proceeds; you can then view the completion of each contract as marking the end of one subsection of the treatment plan and the beginning of another.

As each of these subsections begins, it is useful for you to review the nine 'steps into treatment'. For example, you might review the *intake* data that you first gathered about the client.

Have you learned anything new about her that leads you now to view her differently?

Might it be, even, that you now see a need for *referral*? Such a need could arise simply because she now wants to work with a specialised area for which you are not qualified (e.g. that of eating disorders). Referral, here, might simply mean her visiting a specialist in that area for a few sessions while continuing with you as her main counsellor.

Are your *ground rules* still being followed? Are you and your client still working within the parameters of your original *business contract*?; or do you and your client need to negotiate a new business contract? For example, do you and she need to negotiate and agree on a further number of sessions?

It is always essential to review your *diagnosis* at the beginning of each new stage of the treatment process. This is so for two reasons. First, you will have learned more about your client than you knew at earlier stages. Second, her current diagnosis may well have changed, by virtue of the fact that she has achieved movement in treatment with you.

As the new stage of treatment begins, it may be defined by the negotiation of a new *treatment contract*. Even if the new subsection of the treatment plan is marked off by the client's 'recycling' a treatment issue, it is essential that you and she review the treatment contract. Apart from anything else, if her current diagnosis has changed, then the appropriate contract may have changed also (recall the Treatment Triangle from Part I.j).

Now, on the basis of this updated information, you are ready to work out the next phase of your *treatment plan*, including possible sessional contracts.

Before you embark on the next steps in treatment, it is always a good idea to review the status of the client's *escape hatches*. This is especially relevant if she has somehow seemed 'stuck' (or, in the language of an older day, has been 'exhibiting resistance'). If this has been so, you may find it useful to consider if she has indeed closed the escape hatches congruently. It never does any harm, in that case, to invite the client to repeat the procedure for escape-hatch closure.

The individual session

As you begin each new session with your client, it can be helpful to review the nine steps, in the way I have just described for phases of the treatment process. For example: are you and he still working within an agreed business contract? Are you clear about the overall treatment contract you are working towards with him? Is he clear about it? If so, what sessional contracts might be appropriate? (In Point 8, I shall suggest a style of record-keeping that can be of assistance here.)

Each intervention

At the micro-level, you can review the 'steps into treatment' in a split second before every intervention you make. This becomes an attitude of mind, rather than having to be thought through consciously each time. As you open your mouth to speak, you will already have reviewed questions such as the following:

- Will this intervention keep us within the protective boundaries we have already agreed? (*ground rules*)
- Will it be appropriate to the *diagnosis* of the client that I believe applies at this moment? For example, does it address the proper 'contact door'? (see Point 21)
- How will this intervention help the client to move towards fulfilling the current *treatment contract*?

Key point

'Line up the row of dominoes' before moving to invite specific script change. You can do this by following the nine steps that I have suggested in this Point.

Review these steps regularly as you and your client move through each stage of your work together.

---

4   Set clear and flexible boundaries

In TA counselling, boundary-setting corresponds mainly to setting *ground rules* and negotiating the business contract. My suggestion to you in this Point is: make your boundaries both clear and flexible.

'Clear' v. 'unclear', 'rigid' v. 'flexible'

In everyday language, there is an understandable tendency to equate 'clear' with 'rigid', and 'flexible' with 'unclear'. For example, if I say 'I set a clear boundary', many hearers would assume also that this boundary will not be readily movable – that is, that it will be rigid.

In reality, however, the qualities of 'clearness' and 'rigidity' are different from each other and are mutually independent. So are the respective opposite qualities, 'unclearness' and 'flexibility'.

This lets us realise that boundaries may be of four different kinds. They may be:

* clear and rigid;
* unclear and rigid;
* unclear and flexible;
* clear and flexible.

To illustrate, let us take the example of setting time-boundaries for the beginning and end of counselling sessions.

The counsellor who sets a *clear and rigid* boundary might tell her client 'I'll see you for 50 minutes per session. If you turn up more than 10 minutes late, I'll regard the session as having been cancelled.' If the client arrives 11 minutes late, this counsellor will simply not hold the session. She will close each session 50 minutes from the time she started, irrespective of where the client is at that moment.

A counsellor who sets *unclear and rigid* boundaries may have decided to follow the same inflexible style of using time. However, she will not have made it clear to the client in advance. This counsellor may have spent little time over setting ground rules or negotiating the business contract.

The same will be true of the counsellor who sets *unclear and flexible* boundaries. His clients will also not be clearly told the details of starting time and finishing time, or what will happen if they arrive late. According to how this counsellor feels, sessions may start late, start early, overrun or underrun.

The practitioner who sets *clear and flexible* boundaries will make clear to her clients in advance what is the normal length of sessions, and what rules she usually imposes about late arrival. She may well do this in a written sheet which she hands to prospective clients at the initial interview. She will, however, be ready to renegotiate arrangements or 'bend' rules if the circumstances call for it. This does not reflect any lack of clarity in the rules and contract conditions themselves. Rather, it shows a readiness to employ Adult analysis and make on-the-spot changes if they are to the client's advantage and if she can make these changes without compromising her own protection (recall the 'three Ps' from Part I.k).

The example of co-counselling

A striking example of 'clear and flexible boundaries' comes from a modality other than TA, namely co-counselling (see e.g. Southgate and Randall 1978). In this cooperative approach to personal change, two people typically share a one-hour counselling session. In the first half-hour, person A is the counsellor and person B the client. Then, at exactly 30 minutes into the session, the roles are reversed, with person B stepping into the counsellor role and person A becoming the client.

Note that one aspect of boundary-setting, namely the definition of who is the 'counsellor' and who is the 'client', is completely flexible but also completely clear. Another aspect of boundaries, namely the point in time at which the counsellor and client roles are exchanged, is clear and inflexible. In this instance, the inflexibility is decided upon for a clearly-defined therapeutic purpose.

I have used this example from co-counselling because I think it illustrates well how boundaries can be both clear and flexible. It shows also that flexibility or inflexibility are not 'good' or 'bad' in themselves. The crucial point is that flexibility, or the degree of it, can be decided upon for well-defined ethical or therapeutic reasons.

Rules v. the business contract

I have said that boundary-setting in TA is mainly the province of ground rules and the business contract. What is the difference between the two?

Rules

Rules (sometimes called 'ground rules') are laid down by the practitioner as a prerequisite for the counselling relationship. They are thus *not negotiable*. Essentially, the practitioner is saying to the client: 'I shall only be prepared to work with you if you . . . [*follow this rule*]'. Insofar as the client has scope for choice in his response, it is simply to reply: 'OK, I'll follow the rule and work with you', or 'No, I'm not willing to follow that rule, so I accept that we won't be working together.'

Typical rules set by TA practitioners for the client in individual counselling would be as follows:

- No violence to self or to the other during sessions.
- No damage to be done to the room, fittings or furniture.
- No throwing of hard objects.
- No use of non-prescribed drugs at any time throughout the duration of counselling.
- No attendance at any session while under the influence of alcohol.
- All sessions to be tape-recorded.

For group work, these rules would also typically apply, along with the following:

- Confidentiality to be maintained regarding the work of other group members.
- No sexual relationships to take place between group members, except if that relationship pre-existed the beginning of the group.

Business contract

By contrast, the provisions of the business contract are open to at least some degree of *negotiation* between counsellor and client. Typical points covered in the business contract might be:

- How many sessions will be held initially?
- Will the final session be for evaluation?
- What scope will there be for further sessions?
- What will be the fee?
- At what intervals is it to be paid?
- What will happen if the client misses a session or arrives early or late?

Obviously, there is no completely sharp distinction between rules and business-contract provisions. If, for example, you have a fixed per-hour fee (as I do), then that figure is in itself not negotiable, so might be regarded as a 'rule'. Some practitioners prefer to set few or no rules as such, and to handle even such crucial matters as confidentiality in the form of negotiated agreements.

The important point, I suggest, is to be clear about the conceptual difference between the two, then make your own decision about which matters you are going to deal with in your rules, and which other matters you are prepared to negotiate in your business contract.

Escape-hatch closure must never be a 'rule'

There is one exception to this last suggestion. That is: the closure of escape hatches (recall Part I.1) *must never be set as a rule.*

It might seem unnecessary to specify this, but I have heard more than one trainee practitioner say that he 'would only work with clients who had closed escape hatches'. In such a case, the counsellor is setting escape-hatch closure as a non-negotiable precondition for working with the client – in other words, as a rule.

To attempt to set escape-hatch closure as a 'rule' contravenes an essential feature of closing escape hatches: namely, that it needs to be a decision made by the client from Adult. When a client is just beginning in counselling, it is most unlikely that she would be in a position to make a genuinely Adult decision to accept a 'rule' of escape-hatch closure.

In any case, to attempt to set closure as a 'rule' would mean that the counsellor would not be able to perform her crucial task of witnessing the client's decision and watching for incongruity. I shall say more about closing escape hatches, and the appropriate ways to bring this procedure into the treatment plan, in Point 7.

Key point

Bear in mind that clear boundaries can be flexible, and flexible boundaries can be clear.

Set your own clear boundaries. Decide their flexibility in the light of protection and the therapeutic needs of the client.

---

5   Ask your client to draw up a goals list

In Point 2, I suggested that *effective counselling is outcome-powered*. Thus one of my recommended steps into treatment (Point 3) was to invite my clients to compile a list of their goals for change. In this Point I say more about the nature of goals, their benefits and methods of eliciting them. The bulk of the Point consists of a practical goal-setting exercise.

Problems v. goals

Most people who come to counselling do so with a *problem* they are bringing. Their initial intention then is to 'get rid of the problem'. Or they may wish to 'solve the problem', in which case they will still be left without the problem.

This may make perfect sense from an Adult point of view. To the Child, however, things appear different. Who, asks the Child, wants anything to be *taken away* from them, so that they are left *without* it? Especially when what is to be taken away has been a comforting defence for many years? Small wonder that the Child often takes measures to make sure that the Adult's 'problem' remains unsolved.

Using a goals list at an early stage in treatment gives the person a way of changing her frame on this entire matter. What she focuses on now is not an unwanted problem, but a set of desired outcomes. Instead of the Child facing the loss of something familiar, she can consider what she can get that will be new and different. The person can now 'look forward to the outcome, not backward to the problem'.

As you will realise, this can also be expressed in terms of the three *time-frames* that I discussed in Point 2. Using a goals list helps the person to focus on the changeable future, rather than dwelling on the unchangeable past.

Some people do come to counselling not with a problem, but with a quite specific goal that they want help in achieving. Even in these cases, compiling a goals list can be a helpful step. As you will see, one important component of the goals-list procedure is to *prioritise* different possible goals. The person is thus helped to contextualise the specific want she has brought to counselling: now she has taken time to list this goal against all the other possible goals she might pursue, how high a priority does it turn out to have? What is she prepared to do about it in practice, given that the pursuit of any goal is likely to require time, energy and cost?

Wants v. goals

As a prelude to contract-making, it is important to register the difference between a *want* and a *goal*.

I use 'want' (noun) in its usual conversational meaning. A want, then, is simply a statement of what the person wishes to have or to do, not have or not do. It may often be phrased vaguely or negatively. For example:

'I want to lose weight.'
'I want to be a warmer person.'
'I'd like to not be scared of speaking in public.'
'I wish I didn't have this problem of arguing too much.'

It is usually in this form that people bring their wishes for change to counselling.

Wording of this kind, of course, is a long way from constituting a well-formulated contract in the TA sense. Yet I suggest that it is worth paying close attention to these initial formulations, noting them, and reflecting them back to the person, rather than skipping right over them to 'get on with' working out a full-scale contract. These are typical ways in which the person herself may frame her wants, and as such they are important to her. When you show her you have noted them, you help build rapport. Further, you can often use these initial statements during the process of contract-making to show the client how she may have been sabotaging her own wishes for change by formulating her wants in negative or ill-defined terms.

Converting wants to goals

To convert a *want* to a *goal*, you take the person's initial statement of wants and lead her through a goal-setting process. At a minimum, the process of goal-setting does the following:

1 It engages the person in *listing* her current wants.
2 It has her phrase these wants in *positive words*.
3 It requires her to identify *conflicts* between one desired outcome and another.
4 Thus it requires her to *set priorities* between different possible wants.

Some goal-setting procedures also specify other characteristics for a well-formed goal, for example, that it be phrased in such a way that the person will know without doubt when she has got it, or that it be subject to a stated time limit. However, for TA application the wider definition that I am proposing works better, since these other features are in any case dealt with in TA by the process of contract-making. I define a *goal*, therefore, as 'a want that is phrased in positive words and has been subjected to a check for priority against other wants'.

The goals-list exercise

Following is an exercise that I have found useful as a quick and effective way of helping the person complete a goals list. It is drawn from the work of time-management expert Alan Lakein. I have adapted the exercise from Lakein's excellent book *How to Get Control of Your Time and Your Life* (1973: 30–6).

I shall set out the instructions for the exercise in the form I give them to clients. I hand the client a sheet with the instructions written on it, and ask her to work through them either there and then in the session, or as a working assignment to be completed and discussed at the next session. You may care to do the exercise for yourself now, if you have not already done it. If so, I suggest you read once through all the instructions first.

The goals-list exercise

Set aside about 15 minutes. You will need several big sheets of paper, a pencil or pen, and a watch with a seconds timer.

There is no set of 'right' answers to this exercise. Its purpose is to help you identify and clarify what *you* want.

1 Take the first sheet of paper and write at the top: WHAT ARE MY LIFETIME GOALS?

Start timing. Take exactly two minutes to write down answers to that question. Get down as many words as you can in that time. Do not attempt to censor or evaluate at this stage. Put down everything you bring to mind in the time.

Then take another two minutes to review what you have written, alter it or add to it in any way which you feel makes the list more satisfying to you.

2   Take the next sheet and write at the top: WHAT DO I WANT TO ACHIEVE IN THE NEXT THREE YEARS?

As before, get as many ideas down as you can in two minutes exactly. Then take another two minutes to review, alter or add.

3   Take a third sheet and write at the top: IF I KNEW I WOULD BE STRUCK DEAD BY LIGHTNING SIX MONTHS FROM TODAY, HOW WOULD I LIVE UNTIL THEN?

As before, take exactly two minutes to 'brainstorm' with yourself on this question, then another two minutes to review. (Assume that all arrangements for your funeral, etc., have already been dealt with.)

4   Now spend at *least* another two minutes reviewing the entire set of answers on all three of your sheets together.

This stage is not timed, and you can spend as long on it as you want. Here once again, use this chance to alter, add to or subtract from your overall list on all three sheets so that it becomes even more satisfying to you.

5   It is important that you express all your goals in *positive words* – that is, in terms of what you *will* do, get or achieve. If you have worded any of your goals in negative terms – what you *will not* do, or *stop* doing, or *avoid*, or any other such negative word – change it at this stage so that you put it in positive words. This may often entail you asking yourself: 'What am I going to have *instead of* what I don't want to have?' Or, 'What am I going to do *instead of* the behaviour that I want to stop?'

6   Consider whether there are sharp differences between your lifetime, three-year, and six-month lists. If so, does this tell you anything about what you really want from life?

In a TA framework, the lifetime and three-year lists often contain mainly a mixture of Adult and Parent goals ('To start and maintain a physical fitness programme', 'To make half-a-million pounds'). By contrast, the six-month list often gives an insight into uncensored Child goals ('I'd chuck up work and go on a walking tour round the world').

Once again, make any alterations you wish in your combined list, taking as much time as you like.

7   Look for *conflicts* between goals on any one list and between lists. (For example, the goal of going on a walking tour round the world conflicts with the goal of making half-a-million pounds, though it agrees with the goal of beginning a fitness programme.)

You should regard conflicts as a positive aspect of your lists. By identifying these conflicts, you also register the need to deal with them. Conflicts between goals can be dealt with in either or both of two ways:

- setting priorities;
- making compromises.

8   To set priorities, look down each of your lists in turn. Keep potential conflicts in mind as you do this. Pick out the three most important priorities in your lifetime list and label them A1, A2 and A3. Do the same with your three-year list to get B1, B2 and B3, and your six-month list to get C1, C2, C3. Finally, take a clean sheet of paper and write out these nine objectives. These are your nine priority goals.

9   These are not 'graven in stone'. In fact, especially in the early stages of goal-setting, you will benefit from reviewing and reworking the list through several drafts. Know that effective goals are not static, but are constantly subject to change and revision.

Preview: goals are not the same as actions or contracts

As your client completes the goals exercise, it is well worth while to remind her and yourself that *goals* are different from *actions*, which in turn are different from *contracts*.

A goal is not the same as a contract

Compiling a goals list is not the same process as contract-making. Instead, the goals list is a useful step on the way to making a treatment contract for counselling. I shall explain this point further in Point 9 below, where I discuss the difference between *contracts* and *outcomes*.

Goals are not the same as actions

You will realise that in compiling a goals list, the person may well not say anything at all about what she is going to *do* to achieve her stated goals. In other words, a goal is different from an action. I shall explore this important difference also in Point 9.

Key point

Invite your client to complete a *goals list* early in counselling. The exercise in this Point offers a structured way of compiling a goals list.

   The goals list helps your client to 'pull herself' actively through the process of change. She does this by looking forward to a desired outcome, instead of looking backward to the problem.

---

6   Analyse life-script with a brief questionnaire

In this Point I describe how you can carry out an analysis of your client's script, using a brief script questionnaire.

   When script analysis was in its early days, some TA writers suggested script questionnaires that ran to over 100 questions (see e.g. Berne 1972: 427–35). In modern practice, most transactional analysts prefer to use a relatively brief questionnaire to explore the content of the client's life-script. It may contain only ten or a dozen questions. The answers to it are interpreted and compiled on to a script matrix with the use of further free-style probing and discussion with the client.

Use one questionnaire consistently

In this Point I present my own version of the brief script questionnaire. Other transactional analysts use somewhat different sets of questions. I believe the precise wording of a script questionnaire is not crucial. It is not difficult to invent questions that will call forth information about each part of the script. What is important is that you do many script analyses using *one* questionnaire consistently, and that you then go on to work in counselling with the clients whose scripts you have analysed. This is how you gain the feedback that will let you judge how accurate has been your first assessment of each client's script. This feedback, in turn, will allow you to make any necessary adjustments in the way you interpret future clients' answers to your questionnaire.

'Thinking Martian'

During script analysis you need to 'think Martian'. You must read the covert as well as the overt content of the client's communication. Watch and listen for the sighs, grunts, smiles, grimaces, hand actions, changes of posture and all the other non-verbal clues that convey the client's 'secret messages'.

Listen also for double meanings, puns and slips in the client's choice of words. Bear in mind that the language of script is also the language of dreams. In fact, one of the best ways of developing your effectiveness in script analysis is to work intensively with your own and your clients' dreams.

Be ready to use your intuition about the meaning of all these verbal and non-verbal clues. However, always check this intuition with the client to discover if it 'rings a bell' before you go ahead and write it into the script matrix.

Preparing for script analysis

1 Script analysis with the brief questionnaire usually takes at least 90 minutes. It is best, therefore, if the script analysis session can be booked in advance to run for this time or more.
2 You should equip yourself with:
   - a whiteboard and markers to draw up the initial version of the matrix (you and the client will refine and revise it on the board once you have finished the questionnaire).
   - two blank copies of the script matrix diagram, for yourself and your client.
3 Especially when you are new to script analysis, you may find it useful to have your tape-recorder running during the interview. You can come back to the tape afterwards and listen for script clues you may have missed first time round. For her

part, the client may also find it useful to tape-record the session; she can often gain extra insights into her script by listening to the tape at least once through after the interview.

4   Before beginning the interview, explain the idea of script to your client, if she is new to it. It is important to explain also that script analysis gives a 'past road-map', *not* a statement of 'how you are and always will be' (recall the three time-frames from Point 2).

5   Invite a contract for script analysis. Make clear to the client that this will not be a counselling session; the objective for now is to gather information, not to promote change. Be sure that you have the client's clear agreement to this contract.

6   Throughout the session, be true to your side of the contract and *stay out of counselling*. You have no contract for it. Sometimes, script analysis touches on material that is painful for the client. If this occurs, simply ask the client if she wants to take a break or to discontinue the session. Do not em-pathise and do not confront.

7   When the client is ready, go ahead and ask the questions in the following questionnaire. Do this quite briefly, and keep probing to a minimum. On this first pass, note the client's answers verbatim (or as near verbatim as you can manage when writing longhand). As you do so, *underline* the interest-ing words (i.e. the ones you intuitively judge to be clues to her script). You should make brief notes also of any non-verbal signals that accompany the words.

The brief script questionnaire

Following are the questions in my version of the brief script questionnaire. Comments then follow on the purpose of each question.

1   *What kind of person are you?*

This question is designed to draw out information about the *process* of the script as well its *content* (recall Part I.e).

The *content* of the answer to Question 1 is likely to give initial clues to the person's early decisions about self, others and the world. It may also indicate life position, and the person's most favoured rackets and games.

(As regards *process* information from Question 1, you will be watching for behavioural clues that I shall describe fully in the section below on the Process Model. I suggest, therefore, that for now you simply read through the remainder of the instructions for Question 1, then come back to them after you have read the section on the Process Model.)

Be sure that you ask Question 1 from straight Adult and avoid driver behaviour. Otherwise, the client's response is likely to be a return of your own driver.

Note the client's driver order, as shown by words, tones, gestures, postures and facial expressions. Watch especially for the first few seconds of the client's reply. Drivers are often shown in the pause before any words are spoken. Throughout the interview, re-check your assessment of driver order. This indicates your client's personality adaptation(s). It gives you the accompanying knowledge of open, target and trap doors in the Ware Sequence. Driver order also gives you guidance to the client's process script type, that is, the pattern by which the script is lived out over time.

(Before going on to Question 2, tell the client that you will be asking the following four questions separately for his/her mother and father. Ask also: 'Was there anyone else, actually living in your house with you when you were between zero and seven years old, who was in the role of a parent to you?' If yes, use your judgement as to whether this parent-figure needs to be included in the matrix. If so, ask each of the following four questions for the parent-figure also.)

2   *Give five words to describe your mother/father.*

This is likely to give information on the program, the counter-script, and on injunctions or permissions that were modelled.

3   *When you were a child, and your mother/father was angry at you, what would you have been doing?*

This may give injunctions or counterscript commands (either positive or negative, depending on content). It may also indicate which feelings were prohibited in the family. You may probe, if you like, with 'How did he/she show that he/she was angry?'

4   *When you were a child, and your mother/father was pleased with you, what would you have been doing?*

This usually brings out counterscript (either positive or negative), and may indicate permissions or injunctions. Again, you may probe with 'How did he/she show that he/she was pleased?'

5   *If your mother/father were to write her/his autobiography, and you had to find a title for it, what would that title be?*

This may help to reveal the parents' script themes or payoff. Listen for any indication of depressed or disturbed parents, especially a depressed mother.

6   *In your family, is any story told about your birth?*

This *birth myth*, if any, may indicate early attributions and decisions, and help to explain the client's choice of a life position.

7   (In asking this question, get the answer to each part before going on to the next.) *Have you ever thought you might kill yourself / kill anyone else / go crazy?*

This is to detect the presence of one or more of the tragic payoffs in the script. If the person answers 'yes' to any of the three alternatives, probe to discover the circumstances. What are the here-and-now events to which this client may respond by considering killing or harming self or others or going crazy? Also if 'yes' to any, probe as appropriate 'Have you ever done it / attempted it?'

8   *What will it say on your tombstone?*

This may indicate script payoff and central script theme. It sometimes provides a double-check on process script type.

9   *When things go wrong for you, how do you usually feel?*

This gives a direct check on the client's *racket feelings*. The wording is designed to invite a response from the client in Child, the ego-state from which racket feelings are experienced.

10   *If you keep on the way you are at the moment, where are you going to be five years from now?*

This gives further clues to the script theme and payoff. Listen in particular for clues that the payoff may potentially entail suicide, killing or harming others, or going crazy.
    With some clients, particularly those who have done some personal work before script analysis, answers to this question may reflect a desired movement out of script.

11   *If you were given magic wishes, how or what would you change?*

Depending on content, this may indicate the degree to which the client is script-bound and perceiving self-limiting decisions as the goal of life; or may reveal the Free Child want which underlies the client's scripty behaviour, thus indicating the first step towards a contract for change.

Compiling the script matrix

When you have completed the first pass through the questionnaire, you can begin compiling the script matrix on the whiteboard. I usually begin by putting in the counterinjunctions, then add the program if any. Finally I list the injunctions. I find it is a good idea to keep to the list of twelve injunctions suggested by the Gouldings (recall Part I.d).

Return to the verbatim questionnaire answers, which you got on the first pass. You will use them simply as a *starting-point* in completing the matrix. Now is the time to follow up your intuition about the script implications of each of your client's answers. Take time to probe further into the meaning of the 'interesting words' that you underlined the first time through. Refer back to the notes you took on the client's non-verbal clues.

Check all your intuitive interpretations with your client, and make up the matrix accordingly. Usually you and the client will agree on interpretations that 'make sense' or 'strike a bell' for both of you. If a particular interpretation of yours does not 'feel right' to the client, it is usually best to leave it out, or list it provisionally pending further evidence.

Occasionally you may wish to back your judgement that your client is defending against recognising a particular script message. In this case, go ahead and put it in the matrix anyway, explaining to the client your grounds for doing so.

When you have completed the script matrix to your and your client's satisfaction, copy the completed version on to your blank script matrix diagram while the client does the same on her own blank diagram. Finally, rub the completed matrix off the whiteboard in the client's presence.

Do not expect to get the script analysis perfectly right first time. The initial version of the matrix is only a provisional road-map. It may be redrawn many times over as you work with this client. Make this clear to the client also.

Key point

This Point has described how to use a brief script questionnaire. In your practice of script analysis, choose this or another script questionnaire and use it *consistently* with many clients. This affords you the feedback that will enable you to refine your pickup of script clues.

---

7   Invite your client to close escape hatches – non-routinely

In this Point, I counsel that you should treat *closing escape hatches* as a therapeutic intervention of prime importance. It should be one that you apply with close attention and well-judged timing, in a way most suitable to each individual client. It must *never* be regarded simply as a matter of rote or of 'routine'.

Closing escape hatches 'routinely'

You might wonder, indeed, why anybody should imagine that such an important operation could ever be a merely routine matter. Yet, from my experience as a supervisor, I know that some trainee practitioners have been under this mistaken impression. Why?

My guess is that the error may arise from a misunderstanding of the term 'routinely'. The word turns up in a well-known article by Harry Boyd and Laura Cowles-Boyd, two practitioners who have contributed a great deal to the theory and practice of closing escape hatches. In their article, they recommend that: 'the escape hatches should be closed routinely with *all* patients as early in the course of treatment as possible' (Boyd and Cowles-Boyd 1980: 228; emphasis in original).

In my book *TA Counselling in Action* (Stewart 1989: 84), I quoted the Boyds' article, and echoed their phrase by suggesting that escape-hatch closure should be 'routine practice' for TA counsellors.

In my work as a supervisor since then, I have realised that at least some trainee practitioners have construed the word 'routinely' in a different sense from that in which the Boyds (and I) meant it. What we did mean was that you should invite closure of escape hatches with all clients, *as standard practice*, whether or not the client came with a presenting problem concerning self-harm, harm of others, or going crazy.

What we most certainly did *not* mean was that the process itself was to be regarded merely as a 'routine', in the sense of 'something to be mouthed through by rote'.

Closing escape hatches 'as early as possible'

It may be that the Boyds' other phrase, 'as early in the course of treatment as possible', has also been taken too literally by some readers of their article. I have heard some trainees reporting that they ask all their clients to close escape hatches in the first session. Some have even said that they set escape-hatch closure as a rule: that, in other words, they will only work with a client who says 'yes' to the closure of all three escape hatches at the very beginning of counselling.

In reality, the Boyds' phrase 'as early as possible' means as early in counselling as it is possible for that individual client to carry the process through from Adult with full congruence. Some clients may, indeed, be able to do this in the first session, or in the first few sessions. For others, it may take months or even years before they can get to this point. In such cases, the decision to close escape hatches may be the central change that the person makes in counselling.

Guidelines for closing escape hatches

Whether or not the Boyds' wording, or mine, has been interpreted in the way I am guessing, I am glad here to take the chance to straighten the record. As you consider the place of escape-hatch closure in your treatment plan, I would counsel you to follow three guidelines.

First, you should invite *all* clients, whatever their presenting problem, to close escape hatches at an appropriate stage in treatment. In that sense only, escape-hatch closure could be called 'routine'. However, you should never regard it as a 'routine matter' in any other sense. Closing the hatches will be a crucial step in change for many clients. Therefore, you should handle the process as the important step in treatment which it is. It requires all your professional skill in attending to the client's responses and judging their congruity. This can never be done effectively by simply having the client mouth through a set of words.

Second, you should raise the question of escape-hatch closure at an early stage in treatment. However, it never makes sense to ask for escape-hatch closure before you have established at least a sound working relationship with your client. Above all, *never* attempt to set escape-hatch closure as a 'rule'. The most likely outcome of such an attempt will be that you get an incongruent closure, made from a Child ego-state in which the client is either complying with you or preparing to rebel against you. Thus, what you get is neither a sound hatch closure nor an enforceable rule. (I know I am repeating what I have already said in Point 4, but I think it is worth repeating.)

Third, when you judge that the client is ready, you should invite him to close the escape hatches. When you do so, you may find that the client closes the hatches congruently, quickly and without difficulty. Alternatively, he may refuse, or undertake a 'closure' that you judge to be incongruent. In this latter case, *never* rush ahead to attempted script change. Instead, the open escape hatches become the focus of the work.

Common questions about closing escape hatches

In my work as a supervisor, I am often asked particular questions about the closure of escape hatches. Here are the questions that people most often ask, with my suggested answers.

1   *From what ego-state(s) do people close escape hatches?*

Answer: by definition, the closure of escape hatches is done *from Adult*. In closing the hatches, the person takes an Adult *decision* (and *not* a 'promise' or a 'contract') not to kill or harm self or others and not to go crazy.

You will realise that escape-hatch closure is therefore a special case of what Eric Berne called *social control* (Berne 1961: 160–75). Using Adult powers of decision, the person deliberately takes control and overrides any Child urges or Parent internal commands to kill or harm self or others or to go crazy.

To be sure, Child or Parent ego-states may often 'overhear' the Adult decision, and sometimes react strongly to it (Cowles-Boyd 1980; Stewart 1989: 82–3). I believe that the word 'overhear' is not a metaphor, but describes a literal process of internal dialogue.

It makes no sense to speak of someone having 'closed escape hatches from Adult, but not yet from Child'. Escape hatches, by definition, are not 'closed from Child'. It may well be that some clients, even when they have closed escape hatches, still have suicidal or homicidal material in the content of a Child ego-state. But such material is properly dealt with by means of a *redecision*. This means that the client makes a new decision, *while in a Child ego-state*, to live, to respect the life and safety of others, and to stay sane (Goulding and Goulding 1979: 55–61, 215–40). Such a redecision is completely distinct from the closure of escape hatches.

2   *How can I be sure that the client has closed the hatches congruently?*

Answer: you cannot be 'sure' of this, any more than you can be 'sure' of any other factual observation in life. The most you can do is to use all your powers of observation to watch and listen for incongruities while the client is going through the process (Stewart 1989: 85–90).

Since none of us is perfect, you are likely to be mistaken some of the time. It may be that you will either judge the client to have closed an escape hatch when he has not, or judge him not to have closed the hatch when he has. If in *reasonable* doubt, assume the hatch has not been closed. However, listen also for your own internal dialogue which may be telling you to 'Be Perfect'.

It is important to realise that you can come back to the question of escape-hatch closure at any time in the course of counselling with a particular client. Therefore, if he is showing any signs that you may have mistakenly judged a hatch to be closed, you can ask him to go through the process of closure again, once again looking out for any clues to incongruity.

3   *Who closes the hatches – me or the client?*

Answer: the client does. Further, once the hatches are closed, it is the *client's* responsibility to keep them closed, not yours.

This question is not often asked as baldly as I have just stated it. However, it is sometimes implied when trainee counsellors make statements like: '*I closed* the client's escape hatches in the tenth session.' No, the counsellor did not close the client's hatches; the client did. Or perhaps, of course, the client did not. The counsellor's use of this wording may be a warning sign that she has been coming from a Parental ego-state during the process, and that the apparent 'closure' by the client was in reality done from compliant or rebellious Child.

4 What is the difference between 'hard' and 'soft' closure?

Answer: I suggest that you do not use these phrases at all. So-called 'soft closure' means different things to different people, and there is no agreed definition of the term. Instead, you can note what are the real possibilities that arise when the client is not willing to close the escape hatches fully.

First, what is full closure? It is closure that is (a) *congruent*, and (b) *non-time-limited*. Thus you will realise that if the client does not close the hatches fully, he may offer a 'closure' that fits one of three other types:

1   incongruent and time-limited;
2   incongruent and non-time-limited;
3   congruent and time-limited.

You have a clear response to the first two of these: an incongruent 'closure' counts as no closure at all. It is thus immaterial whether such a 'closure' is time-limited or not.

What about case (3), where the client congruently closes the hatches for a specific length of time in the future? In this case, your action is first to make sure that the time-period the client states is fully specific and unambiguous. (For example, what would you do with the undertaking: 'I won't kill or harm myself or others, or go crazy, at least until our next counselling session'?) If you need to, you can then ask the client to clarify, until you do get an unambiguous statement. You will of course be watching all the while for incongruity.

If you do get a congruent, specific, time-limited closure, then you can proceed as if the hatches were fully closed, for the duration of the stated time-limit. It goes without saying that you need to come back to the question of escape hatches before the stated time-period is up. For this purpose, a large highlighted reminder in your case notes is a good idea.

Key point

The process of closing escape hatches is a crucial element in change for most clients. It calls for the full application of your professional skill and judgement. It is indicated with every client, no matter what her presenting problem. In this sense, and this sense only, can it be called a 'routine' procedure.

8 Keep your case notes as a 'front sheet'

In this Point I suggest that an excellent way to keep your case notes is to lay them out in the form of a 'front sheet'.

What is a 'front sheet'? It is a sheet of information, set out in a structured sequence of headings, that describes the main features of your current work with a particular client. In TA supervision, the trainee will often present a short audiotaped sample of her work, accompanied by a verbatim transcript. As supporting information, she will usually also give a brief written description of the main features of the work that is heard on the tape. She attaches this information to the front of the transcript – hence, 'front sheet'.

My suggestion here is that you can use the front sheet format not only to compile the supporting information on tape samples, but also as an everyday method of keeping your case notes. As your work with a client progresses from session to session, you update your front sheet record.

The front sheet record is a different thing from an *intake* record, and is used for different purposes. I have described a typical intake record in *TA Counselling in Action* (Stewart 1989: 41–3).

Layout of the front sheet

There is no official source that describes a standard layout for the front sheet. However, the layout that follows is typical. It covers all the main points that, in my view, are needed on a competent front sheet.

You should maintain confidentiality for the client by using an initial, or a false name, on the front sheet (and the accompanying transcript and tape, if any).

The headings on my recommended front sheet are as follows:

1 Vital statistics of the client:
  (a) codename or initial;
  (b) gender;
  (c) age;

(d)   current employment;
(e)   current living situation.

2   Working context:
(a)   what was the source of the referral?
(b)   in what setting do you see this client? (if there is a choice, e.g. whether private-practice or within an institution)
(c)   do you see the client in a group or individually?
(d)   length of each session?
(e)   number of sessions completed (or time in counselling) up to the present session?

3   Presenting problem.

4   Diagnosis:
(a)   using any two diagnostic models from TA;
(b)   using a standard diagnostic manual, e.g. DSM-IV.

5   Overall contract.

6   Contract for this session.

7   Lead-in to the work.

8   Nature of the work.

Some of these headings are self-explanatory – the following are some notes on those that need explanation.

Current employment and living situation (1(d) and 1(e))

Enter the facts here as briefly as possible. You can also ask for, and record, some initial detail of how the client feels about both her employment and her living situation. For example: 'Accountant; happy in her work. Lives with partner J. and two children, 5 and 3. Relationship generally OK but some worries over money.'

Presenting problem (3)

This will usually be the problem that the client brought when first referred. In longer-term counselling, when the client may already have made personal changes, the presenting problem may mean the issue that the client is currently working to resolve. You should describe it in brief, using the client's own words or a précis of them.

Diagnosis using two TA models (4(a))

It is usual practice (though not essential) that one of the TA models used is the *script matrix* (see Part I.d). Another model frequently used is the *Racket System*, now alternatively called the *Script System* (Erskine and Zalcman 1979; Stewart and Joines 1987: 220–30; Erskine and Moursund 1988; Stewart 1989: 21–6).

A powerful model for both diagnosis and intervention is the *Process Model* (Kahler 1979a, 1979b), with which is joined Paul Ware's work on *personality adaptations* (Ware 1983). Points 17–24 in this book describe the detailed use of the Process Model.

Other possible diagnostic models are the *discount matrix* (Mellor and Sigmund 1975a; Stewart 1989: 120–6) and the model of *symbiosis* (Schiff et al. 1975).

Diagnosis using a standard diagnostic manual (4(b))

The standard manual most used in TA work is currently the 'DSM-IV' (*Diagnostic and Statistical Manual of Mental Disorders*, 4th edn, American Psychiatric Association 1994). This manual contains detailed guidance on how to use its diagnostic procedures.

If you are in private practice, you will not be working with clients who suffer from the more severe disturbances. This being so, some transactional analysts prefer not to attach formal DSM-IV diagnoses to their clients. They feel this might lead to misunderstanding with other professionals who are used to seeing the formal diagnoses attached only to people who suffer from psychiatrically diagnosable disabilities. A good compromise is to use a form of words such as: 'Axis II: No diagnosis, but *some traits of* Schizoid personality'.

Overall contract (5) and contract for this session (6)

I have outlined the nature and purpose of *contracts* in TA in Part I.i. In Points 9–16, I shall be giving suggestions about the detailed technique of contract-making, including the relationship between the overall contract and the session contract.

I strongly suggest that your front sheet record should list only one overall contract at a time. If you and the client have agreed several different main contract goals, it is best to focus on one at a time, putting the others temporarily 'on hold'. To work for several goals at the same time is to invite the Try Hard driver (see Point 18).

Lead-in to the work (7)

This should be a brief description that sets the scene of the work done in the session (or heard on the tape). A good check-question to ask is: 'If somebody were to listen to this piece of work on tape, without knowing anything in advance about me or the client, what is the minimum I need to tell them about the lead-in so that they will understand from the start what is going on?' Bear in mind that this listener would already have read your description of the client, the setting, the presenting problem, and the overall and sessional contracts. The lead-in description, therefore, only needs to cover points not mentioned under any of these earlier headings.

A typical lead-in description might be: 'I had invited C. to put her father on a cushion in imagination and hold a conversation with him. At the opening of the work heard on tape, C. has changed cushions and is heard speaking as "father".'

Nature of the work (8)

At this heading, give a description of the work in TA terms. It is a good idea to mention:

- the underlying theoretical model;
- the technique(s) you used; and
- the therapeutic outcome for the client.

Some examples might be:

- Decontamination using the discount matrix.
- Early-scene work leading to resolution of a Type II impasse.
- Confrontation of redefining transactions through use of group process.

Using the front sheet record before and after sessions

The front sheet format gives you a concise and structured way of recording each session immediately after it is over. Also, it is an excellent aide-memoire to consult just before you begin your next session with that client. Going through your front sheet in advance of a session, you can both remind yourself what you and the client did last time and envisage what you might do this time.

Obviously, some of the front sheet details will be entered at your first session and will then (normally) never be changed, for example, the client's name. But most of the important items listed on the front sheet relate to aspects of counselling that you will be reviewing after sessions and planning before sessions.

A central point of focus on the front sheet is *congruence*. That is: do the various pieces of information on it 'fit' with each other? Here are some of the questions you might ask yourself as you complete the front sheet record after a session, or use it to plan coming sessions:

1   Is the *setting* for the work still appropriate? For example, might I see the client in a group instead of individually? At a different frequency or for a different length of session?
2   Does my current *diagnosis* of the client still fit what she is presenting now? Or do I need to review or change my diagnosis?
3   Do the details of my diagnosis on the two TA models fit with each other, and with the diagnosis on the standard manual? For example: if I have the client's script matrix containing the injunction 'Don't Make It', does my picture of her Racket System show a *belief about self* that says 'I'll never make it', or something similar?

    Or, if I place the client on the Process Model in the Sceptic adaptation (see Point 19), do the counterinjunctions Be Perfect and Be Strong appear in the script matrix? And does she show at least some trace of the personality characteristics that mark out the Paranoid diagnosis in the DSM-IV?
4   Does my current *overall contract* with the client 'make sense' in the light of the current diagnosis I am attaching to her? (See Point 23 for ways of addressing this important question.)
5   Does the *session contract* clearly further the achievement of the overall contract?

You can ask yourself these questions in retrospect when you are using the front sheet format to review a past session. You can also preview them when you use it to plan a coming session. For example: having considered your current diagnosis and decided you are still satisfied with it, you can check whether the overall contract still seems to be congruent with this diagnosis. Then you can go on to consider what possible session contracts you might invite in the coming session to facilitate your client in completing that overall contract.

Using the front sheet as a tool for self-supervision

The front sheet record is an excellent tool for self-supervision, to help you analyse what goes on in a taped section of work. I strongly suggest that you consider the tape and the front sheet as an integrated whole, not as two separate entities. The interventions and responses heard on the tape can only 'make sense' when you consider them in the light of your current diagnosis, and in terms of the overall contract that you and your client are working to complete.

Here yet again, you may recall the 'Treatment Triangle' (Part I.j). The front sheet record is a good way of keeping a continual check on congruity between the three points of the Triangle: contract, diagnosis and treatment direction.

Key point

Keep your case notes in the form of a 'front sheet'.

Update this record as your work goes on. Use it to keep a continual check on the *congruity* between your contract, diagnosis and treatment direction.

You can use the front sheet as a guide to both short-term and long-term treatment planning. It is also a useful tool in self-supervision.

Contract-making

Contract-making is at the heart of personal change in TA. When you and your client agree a sound contract for change, you have by that token already done most of the work. By contrast, without a well-formed contract, effective change will happen only by accident.

Yet, from my work as a supervisor, I know that contract-making is the most frequent arena for common errors in TA counselling. Why should this be so?

The problem, I believe, is that much of the accepted wisdom about contract-making in TA does not reflect current best practice. In other words, when experienced transactional analysts make effective contracts, much of what they do is different from what the books have said they should do.

My aim in this section is to remedy that mismatch. In these eight Points, I shall suggest guidelines for contract-making that do describe best practice in today's TA. To that degree, what I am suggesting in this section is not 'new'; it is a statement of what effective contract-makers in TA already do.

However, I shall be proposing changes in some familiar principles and definitions. In particular, I shall argue that some of the most important terms traditionally used in contract-making are unclear. Therefore, I shall suggest some new and more precise terms to replace them.

All the ideas and terms I discuss in this section are closely interrelated one with another. I suggest, therefore, that you may find it useful to begin by reading straight through the section (Points 9–16), then come back and consider each Point in more detail.

A preview of this section

I assume that by the time you come to this section, you have already met the distinction between *wants* and *goals* (Point 5). Your interest now is to consider how you and your client can move from goals to contracts.

I begin in Point 9 by questioning Eric Berne's dictum that

workable contracts in TA must always be for *actions*. In practice, this is simply not so. Effective contracts in TA are just as often about *outcomes*. I therefore propose an explicit distinction between *action contracts* and *outcome contracts*.

Point 10 looks at outcomes in more detail. I suggest how you can keep track of multiple desired outcomes, using my model of the *Outcome Matrix*.

Everybody knows that a contract in TA must be 'clear'. But, as Points 11 and 12 go on to ask, what do we mean by a 'clear contract'? The traditional demand in TA has been that the contract be 'behavioural and observable'. But this criterion falls apart when we realise that many fine contracts in TA are for outcomes, not actions. Outcomes are observable, but they are not behavioural. My conclusion in these two Points is: the word 'clear', as applied to a contract, is itself unclear. In its place I propose two new terms to describe an effective contract: it should be *sensory-based* (Point 11) and *finishable* (Point 12).

Many of the client's most important goals in TA counselling will relate to script change. This poses a dilemma: contracts for script change are neither sensory-based nor finishable. In Point 13, I suggest how you can resolve this difficulty by using sensory-based contract statements that I call *markers*.

Point 14 explains how you can keep the contract precise yet *flexible*. In Point 15, I look at an important facet of contract-making that has received little attention in the TA literature until now, namely: what is the *context* in which the client will carry out the contract?

Finally, in Point 16 I describe a visualisation technique to help your client 'bring the contract alive' in his imagination.

9   Distinguish contracts from outcomes and actions

In this Point, I invite you to distinguish clearly between *contracts*, *outcomes* and *actions*. Here are the four main points I shall be making:

- An outcome is different from an action.
- A contract is different from either an outcome or an action.

- A contract in TA may be *either* for an outcome *or* for an action.
- However, if a contract is for an outcome, it must be supported by at least one contract for an action.

In making the third of these points, I am implying a different definition of a 'contract' from the one used by Eric Berne. I shall discuss this further below.

Throughout this Point and the ones that follow, I shall use the words 'goal' and 'outcome' interchangeably.

Outcomes are not the same as actions

As the client completes the goals exercise, you can help him to the important realisation that *outcomes* (goals) are not the same as *actions*.

For example, one of the person's three-year goals may be 'To get a new job'. This says nothing at all about what he is going to *do* to achieve the goal. 'Getting a new job' describes an outcome, not a set of actions.

The next essential step in change, therefore, is to consider some actions that will help him achieve the outcome he desires. For the person wanting to get the new job, a few of such actions might be:

- 'To buy the local paper and read the job adverts.'
- 'To write up my c.v. and have it printed out by an agency.'
- 'To read a book about doing job interviews.'

One obvious difference between outcomes and actions is that outcomes refer to *states of affairs*. Actions, by contrast, refer to *behaviours*.

Another difference relates to the three time-frames of past, present and future (recall Point 2). Action is in the *present*, while outcomes are in the *future*. This is another fundamental distinction between outcomes and actions.

But where do contracts fit into all this? Are they about outcomes, or about actions? And *should* they be about outcomes, or about actions?

Are TA contracts about outcomes or about actions?

You will recall from Part I.i that Eric Berne defined a *contract* as 'an explicit bilateral commitment to a well-defined course of action'. This leaves no room for doubt that, for Berne at least, a contract had *always* to entail agreement on some kind of action.

But what about the goal of that action? On this point, Berne's definition has nothing to say. At most, we may guess that he was implying that the parties to the contract also agreed on a desired outcome. However, this guess may be a dangerous leap of faith.

At first sight it might seem nonsensical to suggest that two people could agree explicitly on a 'course of action' without also agreeing on the *goal* of that action. However, when counselling in TA comes unstuck, this may be precisely because client and counsellor have agreed a contract for a particular course of action, but have different (unstated) ideas about the goal of the action.

A practical re-formulation of Berne

In my experience, the contracts that are made in practical TA often do not conform to Berne's definition. Thus, differing for once from the wisdom of TA's founder, I suggest the following two revised principles:

1 Contracts in TA may be *either* for outcomes *or* for actions.
2 However, any contract for an outcome must be supported by at least one contract for a related action.

I shall go on to explain my reasoning in proposing these two new principles. For brevity, I shall use the phrases *outcome contract* and *action contract* to mean respectively a contract for an outcome and a contract for an action.

Contracts in TA may be either for outcomes or for actions

I make this revision simply because, in practice, the contracts that people agree upon in effective TA counselling are as often about outcomes as they are about actions. Indeed, I shall go further: I suggest that the contracts most crucial to personal change are likely to centre on outcomes rather than on actions.

For example, let us return to the client whose goal is to get a new job. If he and his counsellor agree a contract that simply says: 'I will get a new job within three years', they have not agreed on any action that the client will take. Yet this contract wording goes directly to the client's stated outcome. It speaks of a state of affairs that is different, in a desired way, from the existing state of affairs. Without doubt, it describes a clearly specified, observable change on the client's part. This change takes the form of an outcome, not an action.

The outcome contract must be supported by an action contract

Why must any outcome contract have at least one action contract to support it? There is one immediately obvious practical reason for this. That is: only by *doing* something can the person interact with the world. If my outcome contract is 'To get a new job', I must carry out at least one action to help bring that outcome about. If I do not act, nothing new will happen.

There is one variety of outcome contract where the importance of taking action may not be so immediately obvious. Examples of this kind of outcome contract might be:

- 'To *feel* comfortable when I'm speaking in public.'
- 'To fully *experience myself* as someone who can get close to others.'
- 'To *realise* at all levels of my awareness that I can stay healthy and still get attention from other people.'

In 'feelings contracts' like these, the desired outcome is not itself observable. Instead, it speaks of the client's internal experience. This changed experience may well be the client's most desired outcome, and to that extent it is an appropriate statement of a contract.

Yet if the client does not *do* anything different, then others in the world will have no way of knowing that she is experiencing herself differently. If they do not know this, then they are likely to keep on responding to her in the way they responded before she changed her experience. This in turn may well make it more difficult for her to maintain her desired change.

For example, take the person who wants to 'feel comfortable when speaking in public'. Suppose that she goes ahead in counselling and changes her internal feeling from one of discomfort to one of comfort. However, suppose too that she still *looks* and *sounds* uncomfortable. Her listeners are likely to respond with some unease, just as they did when she still felt uncomfortable. As she notes them looking uneasy, it becomes more difficult for her to maintain her own feeling of internal comfort.

To avoid this difficulty, the client can take one or more action contracts that will demonstrate externally to others (including the counsellor) the internal shift in experience that she has achieved. At the very simplest level, the action contract may simply be to *tell* others about this internal experience.

For example, this client whose outcome contract is 'to feel comfortable when I'm speaking in public' might take supporting action contracts like these:

- 'To role-play making a speech here in the group.'
- 'To make a five-minute presentation in my evening class, and tell you [counsellor] at our next session how I felt while I was doing it.'

Such action contracts take the form of demonstrations that the outcome contract has been achieved (or, is in the course of being achieved). I shall say more about this when I describe *markers* in Point 13.

Action words create action experience

I suggest there is a less obvious, but equally important, reason why effective contract-making demands the formulation of at least one action contract. It is that *words create experience*. Thus, as the client formulates the *words* of an action contract, he must also internally create the *experience* of this change-promoting action.

Sometimes, clients come to counselling with a fairly clear idea of the outcome they want to achieve, but they have not succeeded in achieving it. This is often because they have specified their desired goal, but have not decided upon any action to bring that goal about.

When they do formulate an action contract, they do themselves the favour of starting out on *doing* something to achieve the outcome they have set. What they also do is that, through formulating the words of the action contract, they necessarily reframe their experience of what they *can do* to bring about active change. The 'action words' themselves create a new 'action experience' for the client. That new experience itself is a powerful aid to personal growth. Once again, we see the client grasping a 'handle' and 'pulling himself through' the process of change.

Key point

Effective contracts in TA can be either for *outcomes* or for *actions*.

Where the client's main contract is for an outcome, this *outcome contract* must be supported by at least one *action contract*.

---

10 Keep track of multiple outcomes: the Outcome Matrix

In any negotiation between two people, the possible outcomes under consideration number not two, but *four*.

Why is this so? Because, when you and I negotiate, I have an outcome in mind for myself, but I also háve an outcome in mind for *you*. You, in turn, have an outcome in mind for yourself, but you also have an outcome in mind for *me*.

I have used this realisation to construct a model that I call the *Outcome Matrix*. I have found it useful in clarifying the process of contract-making, particularly when there are more than two parties to the contract. In this Point, I describe the Outcome Matrix and suggest how you can use it.

The Outcome Matrix for two people

Imagine the situation where a client has just come to you for counselling. You have completed the intake process, and have asked the client to make out a goals list so that you can both discover what the client wants to achieve from his work with you. At this time you can generate the simplest form of the Outcome Matrix, a two-by-two model shown in Figure 10.1.

The Outcome Matrix diagram consists of two columns. Each column lists the people (or, sometimes, the groups or organisations) who are taking part in the outcome negotiation. The two columns match each other exactly, except for the headings at the top. The left-hand column is headed 'Outcomes wanted *by*' and the right-hand one is headed 'Outcomes wanted *for*'.

Each box in the left-hand column has arrows running from it to each of the boxes in the right-hand column. Thus each arrow represents an outcome wanted *by* someone *for* someone. The outcome arrows are numbered, simply by taking them in vertical order down the diagram. You can list the content of each outcome, labelled with the number of its arrow, below the diagram or on a separate sheet.

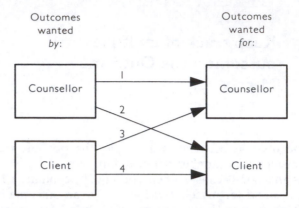

Figure 10.1   *Two-person Outcome Matrix (showing social level only)*

The client's outcome for himself

Naturally, the obvious focus in the first instance will be upon what the client wants to get for himself. In the terms of the Outcome Matrix, this translates as 'the client's outcome for himself'. It corresponds to Outcome 4 in Figure 10.1. The content of this outcome on initial referral will most likely be one of the typical wants that clients bring to counselling, for example, 'to gain confidence', 'to stop arguing so much', 'to lose weight'.

Often in the traditional process of TA contract-making, this is the only outcome that the counsellor and client will concentrate upon. The counsellor may start from the client's stated outcome for himself, and take the client straight into the task of translating the wanted outcome into the terms of a properly stated contract. However, to do so ignores the fact that there are three other outcomes at stake in the negotiation. My experience is that attention to these other outcomes can often enrich the process of contract-making.

The counsellor's outcome for herself

Considering Outcome 1 in Figure 10.1: what is your outcome *for yourself* in this counselling relationship? You may have more than one outcome. It may be 'to earn my fees', 'to avoid litigation', 'to enjoy exercising my professional skills', or many other possibilities.

If you find yourself stating outcomes for yourself such as 'to get this client cured', then you are in fact giving your outcomes for the client, not your outcomes for yourself. I suggest if this is so, it is worth taking some time to establish what your outcomes for yourself actually are.

For this purpose you can use the check question: 'What's in it for me to . . . [e.g. get this client cured]?' You are bound to have outcomes in mind for yourself, no matter how altruistic you are; if you did not have outcomes for yourself in mind, you would not be doing counselling.

By establishing your outcomes for yourself, you put yourself in a better position to ask and answer some important questions. For example:

- 'Now I know what I'm doing this for, do I still want to do it?'
- 'Do I still want to do it in the way I was intending to do it?'
- 'Is the proposed contract with this client a good way of my getting what *I* want to get, as well as the client getting what *he* wants to get?'

This last question may seem an odd one to ask in your role as a counsellor. But I believe that it expresses one of TA's basic philosophical principles: 'I'm OK, you're OK'. The part of the motto at stake is 'I'm OK', where 'I' means the counsellor.

By bringing your own desired outcomes into your awareness, you also lessen the possibility of psychological-level incongruities in your communication with your client. I shall say more about this below.

The counsellor's outcome for the client

Outcome 2 on Figure 10.1 is the outcome that *you* wish for your client. Again, this concept may seem strange at first sight in a traditional TA contract-making context, where the focus has been on asking the client to contract for 'what he wants for himself'. But in reality, the whole process of contract negotiation presupposes that you have outcomes that you desire for your client, and that these outcomes may (at first) differ from the client's desired outcomes for himself. If it were not so, then there would be no need for any process of contract *negotiation*; the contract agreed upon would always be simply what the client first chose to go for. In fact, the bilateral agreement of a contract between you and your client is a confirmation that you have agreed upon an outcome *for the client* that you both wish, or at least that you are both willing to accept.

Why might it be that your outcome for your client would be different from his desired outcome for himself? One obvious reason is that his initially-stated outcome could be one that, in your judgement, was in danger of furthering his script in some way.

For example, a workaholic client might come to you asking you to show her ways to fit yet more work into each day. You might judge that any such contract would simply allow the client to dig herself even more deeply into a 'Work Hard' counterscript. Therefore, your desired outcome for her might be exactly the opposite of her outcome for herself: namely, that she found ways of giving herself permission to work *less* hard. It is from there that your contract negotiation would start.

Again, you might experience the client's initial outcome for herself as being one that was distasteful to you, or that would involve you in some activity that you deemed unprofessional or unethical. For example, she might come to you asking you to help her in selling people more of items which they really did not need. Your outcome for the client in such circumstances might be that she find a different counsellor, or get her needs met in a different way altogether.

The client's outcome for the counsellor

This permutation, shown as Outcome 3 on Figure 10.1, may be the one that is least of all brought into awareness in conventional contract-making. Why, indeed, should the client have any outcome in mind for the counsellor? For sure, the client may be aware that he wants the counsellor to stay around, provide help and show ways in which he can get what he wants from counselling. But these wants describe processes, not outcomes.

Eric Berne suggested an answer to this question. He pointed out that, when most people come to psychotherapy, their wish – outside of their awareness – is that the counsellor should move into a role in their (the client's) script (Berne 1972: 304). This, then, is one way of expressing what the client's outcome for the counsellor may be.

The Outcome Matrix with psychological-level components

I have just pointed out that the client's desired outcome for the counsellor may be held and communicated at psychological

Outcomes
wanted
by:

Outcomes
wanted
for:

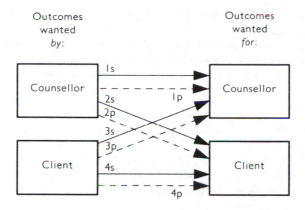

Figure 10.2 *Two-person Outcome Matrix (social and psychological levels)*

rather than social level. This realisation allows us to draw the two-person Outcome Matrix model with psychological-level components. We can again register that each party has desired outcomes for self and for the other. Now, however, we can see that every 'desired outcome' may consist of one outcome that is desired at social level (within awareness) and another outcome that is desired at psychological level (outside of awareness). I have shown these on Figure 10.2 by solid and dotted lines respectively. These do not mean the same as the 'vectors' on a transactional diagram (recall Part I.b), except in that the dotted lines symbolise the psychological level. As before, the arrows simply indicate 'Person A has a desired outcome for Person B'.

Thus, in the simple two-person case, Figure 10.2 confirms that the client has social- and psychological-level desired outcomes for herself and for the counsellor. The counsellor in turn has social- and psychological-level outcomes in mind for himself and the client.

It is the task of script analysis to judge what may be the content of each outcome at the psychological level, for each individual client and counsellor. Some of the innumerable possibilities might be:

- Counsellor for herself (1p): 'To cure this client against all the odds, and so show my internal mother I am OK after all.'

- Counsellor for client (2p): 'That he be a good kid and get cured quickly.'
- Client for counsellor (3p): 'That she produce a Magic Orb from her desk drawer and present it to me.'
- Client for client (4p): 'To find another mother who is better than the first mother I had.'

At an early stage of contract-making with each client, you may find it useful for you and the client each to draw out an Outcome Matrix as in Figure 10.2. You can then compare the outcomes each of you has in mind for self and the other, at both social and psychological levels. Periodically, as counselling goes on, you can repeat the exercise and see how each of the outcomes on the Matrix has changed.

The Outcome Matrix for more than two parties

Often, the counselling contract may be made between more than two parties. For example, wherever counselling is carried on within an institution rather than in 'pure' private practice, there are at least three parties to the contract: the client, the counsellor and the institution. The same is true whenever the client's fees for counselling are being externally financed. You may care to imagine work settings in which the contract is made between even more than three parties.

Eric Berne (1966: 16) wrote penetratingly about the potentially difficult situations that can arise in such situations of multi-handed contract-making. He pointed out that, sometimes, one of the 'hands' in the contract may not be overtly specified at all; for example, the counsellor working in an institutional setting may not have a clear job specification. Whether or not all the 'hands' are specified at social level, Berne pointed out, there is likely to be a 'hidden agenda' for each of the parties at the psychological level.

Berne's prescription was that the practitioner should make sure that she has a clearly stated contract with *all* the parties to her work, preferably in written form. My additional suggestion is that she should also draw out an Outcome Matrix for herself and the other parties. She should fill in both the social-level and the psychological-level outcomes as far as she can discover them. Figure 10.3 shows how the Outcome Matrix would look for a counsellor working in a hospital setting. To avoid overcrowding the diagram, I have included only the arrows that indicate social-

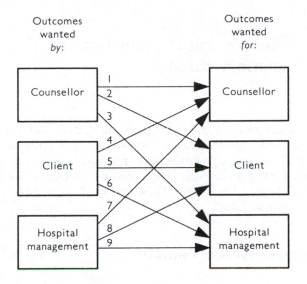

Figure 10.3 *Example of three-party Outcome Matrix (showing social level only)*

level outcomes. However, there will also be psychological-level outcomes at stake for all three parties. You may like to imagine and list the possible content of the eighteen outcomes that go to make up this Outcome Matrix.

Key point

At an early stage in contract-making, draw up an Outcome Matrix for yourself and each of the other parties to the contract.

You can include psychological-level outcomes as well as those at social level.

---

11   Ensure that the contract is sensory-based

In the introduction to this section, I suggested that instead of seeking the traditional 'clear, observable and behavioural' contract, it makes more sense to ensure that your contract is *sensory-based*. But what goes into making a contract sensory-based? And why is this feature important? These are the two questions I shall deal with in this Point.

What is a sensory-based contract?

I learned about sensory-based contracts in TA from the late Laurence Collinson (workshop presentation). He drew his teaching in turn from the work of Richard Bandler and John Grinder in neuro-linguistic programming. Specifically, it relates to the set of linguistic tools that Bandler and Grinder called the *meta-model* (Bandler and Grinder 1975).

An effective contract, suggested Collinson, needs to be sensory-based. This means that the contract should be stated in such a way that we can check its achievement by using any of our five senses. Can we see, hear, physically feel, smell or taste that the contact is being fulfilled? If yes, the contract is sensory-based. If no, it is not.

In describing the five senses, I used the term 'physically feel' rather than simply 'feel'. This is to stress that 'feel', here, equates to 'feel physically', not 'feel emotionally'. You will see the significance of this from the following familiar dialogue:

> *Counsellor*: So how will you and I know that you're 'getting closer to people' in the way you want to?
> *Client*: Oh, I'll just feel closer to them.

'Sensory-based' is different from 'behavioural'

'Sensory-based' does not necessarily mean the same as 'behavioural'. Take, for example, the contract that we have already met as an example in earlier Points: 'I will get a new job within three years.' This statement is sensory-based. Anyone can see or hear whether or not the person making it has or has not got a new job by the stated time. But it is not behavioural: the phrase 'get a new job' designates an outcome, not an action.

This takes us back to the distinction I made in Point 9 between outcome contracts and action contracts. The contract to 'get a new job' is an outcome contract, not an action contract. What we can realise now, therefore, is this: outcome contracts, as well as action contracts, can be sensory-based. Or, to put it in another way: a contract can be sensory-based without necessarily being behavioural.

Admittedly, in order to get her new job, the person in our example will need to engage in many different appropriate actions (e.g. writing a c.v., giving in her notice to her old job, looking up job advertisements, etc.). Any of these actions might itself become the subject of an action contract. These action contracts would be *both* behavioural *and* sensory-based.

It is obvious, in fact, that any statement of a specific behaviour must be sensory-based. Thus a 'behavioural contract', in the traditional TA sense, must always be a sensory-based contract. What I am suggesting in this Point is that there are many other workable contract statements that are sensory-based, but not behavioural. It is the fact of being sensory-based that is crucial to effective contract-making.

Why is it important that the contract be sensory-based?

Why should it be essential that a contract be phrased in sensory-based terms? The answer is that only a sensory-based contract allows us to achieve some of the main benefits of contractual method. These purposes are as follows.

First, by working contractually, you and your client aim to agree the goals and methods of treatment *mutually and explicitly*. As you will realise, you can only 'agree' something with your client if you both know unambiguously what it is you are agreeing to. It is only through a sensory-based statement that you can be sure of doing this. In other words: you and your client can only agree on something if you both know in detail what you will be seeing, hearing and physically feeling when that event takes place.

A second purpose of contractual method is that both parties will know when their work together has been completed. That will be the point at which the client has achieved her contractual goal. From what I have already said, it will be obvious that this aim also can only be realised if the contract statement is sensory-based.

There is a third benefit of contractual method, less often stressed in the classic literature of TA but in my opinion one of the most important. It is that the statement of the contract goal acts as a *visualisation* for both you and your client. It helps you both to construct a mental set that empowers the achievement of that goal. It is characteristic of all visualisation techniques that the more rich the visualisation in sensory detail, the more effective is the technique likely to be. Thus, a sensory-based contract achieves this benefit to the fullest possible extent. (In Point 16, I shall describe a visualisation exercise that you can use in contract-making.)

What features prevent a contract from being sensory-based?

Here are some check-points by which you can judge whether a particular statement is *not* genuinely sensory-based. By a process of elimination, you can then judge what other statements are sensory-based.

At first sight, it might seem only necessary to ask the general question: 'Does this statement denote something that can be seen, heard, felt, tasted or smelled?' Indeed, this is always a useful question to start with. The answer 'No' indicates that the statement in question is *not* sensory-based.

However, words are not the events they portray, and it is in forms of words that the possible pitfalls lie. The check-points that follow are all designed to highlight wording that *seems* to relate to sensory observation, but in fact does not.

Unspecified adjectives

For example, how about the statement 'I will become a friendly person'? At first sight, this may seem to be sensory-based: surely anybody can see, hear, or physically feel whether a person is or is not being friendly?

But in fact, they cannot, because the adjective 'friendly' can

mean different things to different people. To me, 'friendly'
behaviour may mean shaking hands on meeting. To you, it may
mean hugging and passing warm compliments. Thus your
sensory tests would be for a whole different set of criteria from
the ones I use. Some other unspecified adjectives, familiar from
the arena of contract-making, are 'warm', 'close', 'successful' and
'confident'.

You can check for this kind of vagueness, during the process of
contract-making, by asking two questions – one of yourself, the
other of your client. The question to ask yourself is: 'As the client
says this word, is there a chance that she could be seeing, hearing
or feeling something different in her head from what I am seeing,
hearing, or feeling?'

If the answer to that question is 'yes' or 'maybe', then you can
go on to put the second question to your client: 'So when you've
got what you want, how will other people know you've got it?'

As the client answers, check her further answers in turn for
unspecified adjectives. If you hear any, ask the same question
about these words in turn. Continue to ask the question until the
client gives you a sensory-based statement of what it is that
others will see, hear, or physically feel when she has achieved the
change she wants.

It may often also be useful to ask the same question, but
ending: 'how will *you* know you've got it?' In the same way as
before, continue asking the question until the client gives a reply
that expresses how she herself will employ her five senses to
check whether or not she has got what she wants.

Nouns used for verbs

Not only adjectives are subject to this kind of vagueness. The client
may often use nouns like 'feedback', 'decision', 'options', 'help',
'success', 'relationship' or 'comfort'. The common factor among
nouns like these is that they denote not *things* but *processes*.

If you hear this turn of phrase, you can elicit the client's
interpretation of the word by asking him a question that draws
his attention to the verb underlying the noun. For example:

- 'What do you want me to do, so that you know you're
  getting the kind of *feedback* you'll find useful?'
- 'What do you need to find out in order that you can make the
  choice you want to make?'
- 'When you've made this *decision*, how will I know that from
  the way you are behaving?'

Unspecified verbs

Verbs themselves may be non-sensory-based. Examples are 'discuss', 'help', 'feed back', 'experience', 'decide', 'work on' – and, particularly relevant to contract-making – 'feel', when the 'feeling' referred to is anything other than a physical sensation.

Here again, the clarifying response from you is to ask the client to define the non-sensory verb in sensory-based terms, and to stay with this line of enquiry until you and the client know what you and she will be seeing, hearing and feeling as her outcome is fulfilled. For example:

> *Client*: I want to feel comfortable when I'm talking to my boss.
> *Counsellor*: OK. So, when you do feel comfortable when you're talking to your boss, how will you know you're feeling comfortable?
> *Client*: Beg pardon? How do you mean, 'how will I know?'
> *Counsellor*: Well, you told me that up to now, you haven't been feeling comfortable talking to her. Now you want to feel comfortable. So, how will you know that you're feeling comfortable instead of not feeling comfortable?
> *Client*: [*pause*] Well, I'll know it because I'll feel more relaxed inside.
> *Counsellor*: Where inside? Where in your body will you feel that?
> *Client*: Here. [*Indicates mid-line of stomach.*]
> *Counsellor*: There. [*Indicates same place on self.*] OK, so go ahead and let yourself feel that feeling of 'comfort' now. What are you actually feeling there? Are you feeling warm, or are you feeling your muscles going more relaxed, or what?
> *Client*: [*pause*] It's that I feel the muscles getting more relaxed.

You might then go on to ask how *you* would know that the client was 'feeling' the way she wanted to feel. The answer might refer to different observable behaviours, for example talking distinctly rather than muttering, looking you in the eye instead of avoiding eye-contact. Sometimes, the best external indicator to agree upon is that the client can accurately identify the internal difference in physical experience and can report that to you each time she experiences it.

Overgeneralised references

Another frequent reason why a statement is *not* sensory-based is that it uses a generalised term like 'people', 'others', 'friends', 'colleagues', and so on, without specifying who in particular is meant. For example: 'I will make eye-contact with people.'

Without knowing *which* people the client has in mind, you have no way of checking whether or not the contract statement is sensory-based. A clarifying question from you could be: 'Which people are you talking about?' Once again, stay with the client until he has come to a clear statement of which people he means. One useful way of identifying these people is simply to name them.

Of course, once you both know which people the client means, you still have to work out how often and in what circumstances the client is going to make eye-contact with them. These questions are about the *finishability* and *context* of a contract. I shall explore these two subjects in the following Point and Point 15.

Key point

An effective contract in TA must be *sensory-based*. That means that you must be able to see, hear, physically feel, or smell or taste that the contract is being achieved.

---

12 Invite contracts that are finishable

In this Point, I highlight yet another aspect of contract-making that is part of 'best practice' in today's TA, but has not been fully explored in the TA literature until now. It is this: for effective contract-making, you should invite contracts for goals or actions that are *finishable*.

'Finishable' v. 'non-finishable' contracts

The terms 'finishable' and 'non-finishable' are my own. They do not appear in any earlier TA sources. Like all the other words I have used in this section of the book, these have their usual conversational meanings. When you think of various goals or actions for which people may make contracts, you can confirm that some of these goals or actions can be clearly *finished*. Others cannot be clearly finished, and it is this latter class that I call *non-finishable*.

It is perhaps easier to understand this distinction from examples than from definitions. Here are three examples of finishable contracts:

- 'To change my job.'
- 'To go for a bus ride on my own.'
- 'To say hello to two people at work today.'

Here by contrast are three statements that refer to the same content but are non-finishable:

- 'To look for a new job.'
- 'To go for bus rides on my own.'
- 'To say hello to people at work today.'

You can confirm first that all six of these statements are sensory-based (recall Point 11). It is possible to check by seeing, hearing or physically feeling whether a person has got a new job, and you can check in just the same ways whether he is looking for one. The same check applies to the other two pairs of statements. (Though the third statement uses the unspecified noun 'people', you could verify by sensory checking whether these are or are not 'people at work'.)

Let us now compare the first statement in the two sets of examples. If someone takes a contract to 'change her job', then when she does change her job the contract is clearly *finished*. If, by contrast, she takes a contract to 'look for a new job', we have no way of knowing when that contract will be finished. How long does she have to keep on looking in order to know that she has looked enough?

In this example, you might suggest: 'The contract will be finished when she gets a new job, and so stops looking.' However, the original contract statement was not to '*get* a new job'; it was to '*look for* a new job'. It is that feature of wording that makes the contract non-finishable.

Likewise, when a person contracts to 'go on a bus ride', then his contract is finished when he goes on that (one) bus ride. However, a contract to 'go on bus rides' is non-finishable, since we do not know from the contract statement itself *how many* bus rides the person needs to go on before he will count it as finished.

Again, it might be possible to argue around this difficulty by suggesting that as soon as the person has done at least two bus rides, the latter contract is finished. But this does not change the fact that the contract in its original wording is non-finishable. If we assume that just two bus rides are 'enough', then we are attempting to read the client's mind.

Hanging comparatives

A particularly common form of non-finishable contract is one that contains a *hanging comparative*. This is a form of words in which the person appears to be comparing one thing with another, but does not give a standard by which the comparison is to be judged. Examples that come up often in contract-making are:

- 'I will make *more* friends.'
- 'I will get *slimmer*.'
- 'I will get *closer* to my partner.'

Even when you translate the rest of the words in each sentence into sensory-based terms, the hanging comparative would mean that there can be no sensory-specific criterion for the *completion* of the contract. Such statements, therefore, turn out to be non-finishable.

You might suggest that, for the client who was setting out to 'make more friends', the contract would be complete when he had made just one more friend. But so long as the hanging comparative 'more' remains in the statement of the contract, it can literally never be completed. No matter how many friends the client may make, his stated goal is always to make even 'more'.

Why is it important for a contract to be finishable?

At first sight, distinctions like these may seem to be mere 'playing with words'. In a sense, that is precisely what they are, and that is why they are so important.

The late George Thomson used to have a slogan: 'The Child is a careful grammarian' (Thomson, workshop presentation). What he meant was that in your Child ego-state, you have the ability to grasp what words *do* mean, rather than what they are 'supposed to mean' in polite company. Always, the Child resists script change while at the same time welcoming it. If the ingenious use of words enables the Child to slither out of an apparent commitment to change, then she is likely to take grateful advantage of this opportunity.

The 'forever contract'

Mary and Robert Goulding (1979: 80–1) warn therapists of what they call 'forever contracts'. For example, a client may begin therapy by saying: 'I want to *work on* . . . [some problem or other]'. As the Gouldings point out, this wording is a Child device that means exactly what it says: the client will go ahead and 'work on' the problem. But he will not solve it. If he were to solve it, he would no longer be able to work on it.

In the language I am using here, the Gouldings' 'forever contracts' correspond to non-finishable contracts. The Gouldings' warning, therefore, underlines one reason why it is important for a contract to be finishable: any non-finishable contract may be a Child strategy to avoid script change.

Contractual method and finishable contracts

Another reason, this time purely practical, relates to the benefits that are available from using contractual method (recall Point 11). One of these benefits, both for counsellor and client, is to be able to tell unambiguously when their work together is complete. As you will see, it is only by taking a finishable contract that you and your client can realise this benefit.

Achieving finishable contracts

To detect a possibly non-finishable contract statement, you can simply ask yourself the check question: 'How will anybody know when the client has finished doing this?'

If the answer is 'There's no way of knowing', then the contract as stated is non-finishable. Bear in mind that you need to ask the check question about the contract statement *as the client has worded it*, no more, no less. Beware of any tendency on your part to 'read in' criteria of finishing the contract that the client herself has not clearly stated.

When you do detect a non-finishable statement, you can invite the client to think up a finishable version of it by asking her that same check question, reworded as appropriate to fit the specific content of her desired contract. For example:

* 'Will you say *how many* bus rides you're going to do on your own, so you and I will know clearly you've got what you want?'
* 'You say you want to make more friends. How many new friends will you need to make, so you will know you've got the contract we're talking about?' (Obviously, you would also

find out in this example how the client and the others would see, hear and feel that they were 'friends'.)

- 'When you and I have finished "working on" this problem you're bringing, what do you want to have changed in your life?'

Key point

Be aware of the difference between finishable and non-finishable contract statements. If the client suggests a non-finishable contract, invite her to change it to one that is finishable.

---

13   Agree markers for script change

A central goal of change in TA is *movement out of script*. I shall suggest in this Point that this poses a dilemma for you in the process of contract-making. I shall go on to describe how you can resolve that dilemma, using contract statements that I call *markers*.

Making contracts for script change: the counsellor's dilemma

What is the dilemma that you face when you set out on contract-making for script change? An example will best explain it.

Suppose you have completed script analysis with a client. You and she have agreed that one of the limiting injunctions in her script has been 'Don't Be Close'. You therefore agree that your work together will centre on her making a new decision that it *is* OK for her to get close to others.

You next take time with her to work out a positively-worded statement of the script change she wants. She might phrase it in words like these: 'I will redecide my childhood decision to not be close, and I will get close to others.'

At this point, you can see the beginnings of your dilemma. The client's statement of desired script change is neither *sensory-based* nor *finishable*. Therefore, as it stands, it is not a way of wording an effective contract, for all the reasons I have discussed in Points 11 and 12.

Yet it *is* a true statement of the client's broad goal in counselling. It goes to the heart of the main personal change that she wants to make. In Point 5, I suggested that it was important for you to take note of your client's broad wants as she first phrases them, and to reflect back to her that you understand and account these wants. This client's want for script change is no exception.

So what do you do at this point? You are faced with what seems to be a choice between two unsatisfactory options. One is to go ahead and ask your client to replace her initial broad statement with a specific contract that is both sensory-based and finishable. Yet if you take this option, you risk losing sight of the client's central wish for change, of which the narrower contract is merely an illustration.

Your other option, it seems, is simply to accept the client's initial broad 'statement of want' as it stands. You might then accept that statement as the 'overall contract'. If you take this choice, you are certainly accounting the importance of the client's own stated want. But from then on, you and she will be 'flying blind'. You and she will have no clear way of knowing whether, or how, she might ever complete her wanted script change. That is the other side of your dilemma.

Markers for script change

You can resolve this problem by taking a third option. It is to ask your client to state what I call *markers* (Stewart 1989: 101). I define a marker as: 'a sensory-based, finishable contract statement which demonstrates that the client is achieving a broader script change'.

The marker *does not replace* the client's broader statement of script change. Instead, it stands beside it. The client's original, broad want remains the central focus of change. The marker then acts as a tangible indication that she is getting the change she wants.

For example, consider again the person whose desired script change is: 'I will redecide my childhood decision to not be close, and I will get close to others.'

Some of the possible markers might be:

- 'To be in a live-in relationship by . . . [date].'
- 'To have three or more friends that I meet at least once a month.'

- 'To join two clubs in my neighbourhood.'
- 'To write letters to three of my relatives.'
- 'To tell my partner something I like about her every day for a week.'
- 'To put my mother on a chair in imagination and express to her how I feel about her forbidding me to be close to others.'
- 'To talk through with you [counsellor] the ways in which I've been playing a Kick Me game, and work out how I can get what I want without playing the game in future.'

Markers can be for outcomes or actions

So long as the marker is sensory-based and finishable, it can be in the form of *either* an outcome contract *or* an action contract (recall Point 9).[1] In the examples above, the first two are outcome contracts and the remainder are action contracts. As always, if you agree a marker that is an outcome contract, you must also agree at least one action contract to support it.

Markers can be out-of-session or in-session

You will also see that the fourth and fifth examples are of markers that the client agrees to perform between counselling sessions. These out-of-session markers correspond to what are called 'homework assignments' in more traditional language.

Whenever you take an out-of-session marker, you must of course also agree with the client that she is going to report to you about it. Otherwise, it would not be sensory-based as far as you are concerned.

The last two examples are of markers that the client agrees to carry out during the counselling session, that is, in-session markers. Such a marker is the same thing as a *session contract*. Frequently in script-change work, you will agree a series of session contracts that are markers for the overall change that the client is seeking.

---

1 This is different from what I said in *Transactional Analysis Counselling in Action* (Stewart 1989: 101). I suggested then that markers *always* had to be 'behavioural'. At that time, I had not fully realised that contracts can be sensory-based and finishable without necessarily being behavioural. The account I give here supersedes the one in my earlier book.

Formulating a valid marker

Any one script change may generate a large number of possible markers, as in the example I have just given. But how can you judge whether a particular behaviour is a valid marker for a given change in script? You can do so by asking yourself (and your client): 'If you do *this* [i.e. the possible marker], will you be showing clearly that you are achieving the script change you want?'

Since this is a question about observable reality, it can never be answered for certain. Instead, you and your client can agree an Adult judgement in terms of probability. If the answer is 'Yes, if I do *this* behaviour, it will pretty surely mean that I'm moving some way towards fulfilling my script change', then you can judge that the behaviour in question is a valid marker for that contract.

Markers and the 'front sheet'

If you think back to Point 8, you will recall that the standard front sheet contains headings for the 'overall contract' and the 'contract for the session'. I have just suggested that the contract for the session can usually take the form of a marker. (As a rule, this session-contract marker will be for an action rather than an outcome.)

But how about the overall contract? In your choice of words for this important contract, you face the same apparent dilemma as I have just described for contract-making generally. Do you phrase the overall contract in the words of the broad script-change statement that the client herself has chosen? If so, you would seem to be stuck with an overall contract that is neither sensory-based nor finishable. (In traditional language, it would be 'neither behavioural nor measurable'.) That would be true, for example, in the case of the client whose overall want was to 'redecide my childhood decision to not be close, and to get close to others'.

What if you decide instead to go for an overall contract phrased in terms that are sensory-based and finishable? You may then end up with a narrower statement that does not succeed in expressing the 'overall' change the client wants to make. An example would be the contract: 'I will be in a live-in relationship by . . . [date].' Important as this outcome is for the client, it does not say much about the main script change she wants to make.

Does she want her new relationship as a way of affirming that she can be close to others, or that she is important, or that she has grown up, or . . . ?

Phrasing the overall contract as 'script change plus marker'

I suggest that you can resolve this difficulty by phrasing the overall contract as a *two-part* statement. This will consist of:

1   A reference to the part of the script that the client is contract-
.   ing to change; *plus*:
2   A statement of one important *marker* that will demonstrate that the script change has been achieved.

Thus in summary we get:

OVERALL CONTRACT = (SCRIPT CHANGE) + (ONE IMPORTANT
MARKER)

In the example I have been using, the *overall contract* might thus say: 'I will redecide my childhood decision to not be close, and I will get close to others. To mark this, I will be in a live-in relationship by . . . [date].'

Because the important marker here is an outcome contract, you would need also to agree action contracts to help bring about that outcome. Each of these action contracts could itself be a marker for the script change. You might well list one of these markers as the *contract for the session* on your front sheet. For example: 'I will put my mother on a chair in imagination and express to her how I feel about her forbidding me to be close to others.'

Here are some more examples of overall contracts stated as 'script change plus marker':

• 'I will change my childhood decision not to succeed, and I will be successful in my career. To mark this, I will get promotion in my job within 18 months.'
• 'I will move out of my old restrictive decision that I am not important. To celebrate my own importance, I will join a public-speaking class and I will give a speech in public within the next three months.'
• 'I will take a three-week holiday before next Christmas, even if I still have work to finish. In that way I will show that I have an option other than my parents' prescription of "Work Hard".' (This example has the marker coming first in the wording.)

Using markers to evaluate the client's want for change

Clients state their initial 'wants for change' in many different ways. Some of these statements later turn out to be a workable foundation for an overall contract, others do not. Using the idea of markers, you can run a useful advance test on any stated want, to see whether or not it will 'work' as the basis of a contract. The test is as follows: if the client's 'statement of want' *generates at least one sensory-based, finishable marker*, you will be able to use it as the basis of a workable overall contract – if not, not.

For instances of stated script-change wants that do pass this test, you can look again at those I have given in the examples earlier in the Point.

But, you might ask, how could there be a 'statement of want' that does *not* generate at least one marker? This is better answered by examples than by definition. Here are some statements of want that do not generate any markers:

- 'I will be myself.'
- 'I will live my own life.'
- 'I will be a warmer person.'
- 'I will leave my scare behind.'

The first two of these statements are truisms; it is impossible for anyone *not* to 'be herself' or 'live her own life'. The third statement contains a hanging comparative, so there is no marker that can ever show the contract has been finished. The final example is a negative, and so by definition cannot generate any sensory-based markers. You may like to play around further with these ideas, working out further statements of want that do or do not generate markers.

Key point

As part of contract-making, agree *markers*. These are sensory-based, finishable contract statements which demonstrate that the client is achieving a broader goal for script change.

On your 'front sheet', it is often useful to phrase your *overall contract* as 'script change plus one important marker'.

Every *session contract* can itself be a marker.

---

14 Keep the contract clear and flexible

In this Point I suggest that in your work with each client, you should keep your contract *flexible*.

You will recall from Point 4 (on 'Boundaries') the four-way comparison I made between the notions of 'clear' and 'unclear', 'rigid' and 'flexible'. I suggested that it was easy to take for granted that a clear boundary also had to be rigid, and that a flexible boundary also had to be unclear. I argued that in reality it is possible for a boundary to be clear *and* flexible. In this Point, I apply this same reasoning to contract-making.

The meaning of 'flexibility' in contract-making

In the earlier Points of this section, I have suggested that the traditional idea of 'a clear contract' is itself unclear. I have proposed the two terms *sensory-based* and *finishable* as more precise ways of describing a contract that can be called 'clear' in TA terms.

So what do I mean by saying that a contract is 'flexible'? I mean simply that you and your client can *change* the contract at any time.

You will notice that I did not speak only of 'the client changing the contract'. In fact, the initiative to change a contract – like the initiative to offer one in the first place – may just as well come from you as from your client.

Given that the concept of a flexible contract is simple to understand, there arise three questions that are worth discussion:

1 What are the benefits of keeping the contract flexible?
2 What can you do in practice to ensure that your clear contract remains flexible?
3 In what circumstances is it *not* appropriate to change the existing contract?

Why keep the contract flexible?

Counsellors from other disciplines have sometimes been worried about TA's focus on clearly-defined contracts. They have felt that these might act as a hindrance to the client's natural flow of growth. Would it not be more respectful, they have suggested, if the counsellor were simply to allow the client to generate her own ways forward from moment to moment? Surely this is better than narrowing down the route to change by tying it to one specific contract goal?

These concerns are allayed by realising that contracts in TA can be *flexible* while still being clearly specified. As the client grows, so the contract can grow with her. It is your job as counsellor to make sure that this is what happens. One of your prime tasks is to be aware from moment to moment of the potential for *changing* the active contract, while still keeping that contract clearly stated and clearly agreed.

This realisation that 'clear can be flexible' can also help TA counsellors in training. Often, they share the concerns that I have just discussed, about 'contracts hindering natural growth'. Because of an understandable wish to allow the client full freedom in deciding his own route to change, the trainee may be tempted to agree a contract that is stated in unclear terms. What I am suggesting in this Point is that there is a better means of achieving this freedom for the client. It is to work out contracts that are 'clearly' stated – that is, sensory-based and finishable – yet are open to change from moment to moment.

Flexible contract-making in the long and the short term

I suggest it is useful to consider the flexibility of contracts over two different time-scales:

1   Over the longer perspective of the entire treatment plan.
2   In the short term, i.e. from session to session and from moment to moment during a session.

To an extent, this division into long- and short-term flexibility is arbitrary. However, these two aspects of flexibility do raise different questions in practice.

Flexible contract-making within the longer-term treatment plan

In what circumstances is it appropriate to change the contract in the longer term as you carry through your treatment plan? Or, to ask the same question in another way: when is it appropriate to change the overall contract?

One obvious reason for changing the overall contract is that the client has just achieved his overall contract goal. If this is clear to the satisfaction of both you and your client, then you can stroke the client for his achievement and move on to a new contract, or to termination (Stewart 1989: 12–13).

The situation is less clear when the client expresses a wish to change the overall contract *before* he has achieved it. This may be because he has become aware of a change in his set of goals. He may report that his original contract goal now appears less important to him than when he began counselling, or that he has changed the priorities he has attached to different goals. Or he may simply now feel that the contract goal he has been pursuing no longer merits the time and effort he may need to devote to achieving it.

You have a potentially delicate task here. You need always to be open to the possibility that the client may rearrange the priorities of his goals, abandoning some goals and discovering others that he may not even have envisaged before counselling began. Indeed, you would expect that this would be likely as the client grows during counselling. It would be anti-therapeutic for you to attempt to constrict this process of growth just to satisfy a wish to keep the overall contract 'neat'.

At the same time, you have to remain aware of the client's Child inclination to resist change in the script. A request from the client to change or abandon a contract may always represent such 'resistance'. Of course, in Child he will be framing this not as 'resistance' or 'sabotage', but as an urgent attempt to cling to strategies that seem essential to getting his needs met, or even to his survival.

Therefore an essential check question to ask yourself, and your client, before changing or abandoning an existing contract, is: 'What is the chance that this change in contract would further the client's script?'

You can never know the answer to this for certain. However, here are three points that you can use for guidance. First, the client's *goals list* (recall Point 5) can be of further value here. Suppose the client now says he has changed the priorities of his goals, and thus wants to change or abandon a contract. You can go back with the client to the goals list, and have an explicit discussion of how his goal priorities have changed. This may help you and the client judge how far such a change is scripty, and how far it is autonomous.

Second, observe your client's *process* as he talks to you about the possible change in contract. How far do you see and hear his discounting? In particular, how much driver behaviour does he show (see Point 17)? The greater the intensity of redefining and discounting, and the more the driver behaviour, the more likely is it that the request for a contract change is scripty.

Third, be especially cautious about requests for contract change that come just when you were expecting the client to achieve some important *move out of script*, for example a major redecision. As I have already mentioned, the client in Child is likely to experience the potential script change as a threat to the satisfaction of needs, or even to survival. Therefore, it is no surprise if the client inexplicably becomes 'tired of' the current contract goal at such a point in treatment, or suddenly discovers that a new line of change is demanding his energy. It may be advisable for you to confront the possible abandonment of the script change the client was about to make, while at the same time offering appropriate protection for the Child.

Flexible contract-making in the shorter term

How about flexibility in the shorter term, from session to session and from moment to moment within a session? This is mainly a question of how the session contract can be changed over the short term, while still serving the fulfilment of the overall contract.

It is worth recalling that the traditional term 'session contract' does not necessarily mean 'a contract taken for one session and for the whole of that session'. Just as often, it means 'a contract taken within a session'. In the space of any one counselling session, lasting 50 minutes or however long, *many* 'session contracts' may be offered, accepted, declined, completed, abandoned or changed.

This is an area in which you have room for a considerable amount of elegant manoeuvring. To be working contractually, there are only two conditions that you need to be sure are satisfied at every moment:

1 You and your client must have made it explicit to each other what you are doing together.
2 You must both have explicitly agreed to it.

Recall also that you, as well as your client, can *offer* contracts from moment to moment. You do not always have to ask the client for *his* ideas. Indeed, Bob Goulding (workshop presentation) has suggested that it can be a cop-out on the counsellor's part to ask the client 'how' he wants change to be brought about. The 'how', says Goulding, is up to the facilitator to decide; the client only needs to say *what* change he wants.

Thus from session to session and from moment to moment, there is endless scope for both you and the client to be proactive in offering session contracts, all of which can be in the service of the current overall contract.

Key point

You and your client can renegotiate your treatment contract at any time during the process of counselling. In this way, the contract remains *flexible*.

This flexible contract can and should still be 'clear' – that is, *sensory-based* and *finishable*.

---

15   Put the contract in context

In this Point I recommend that for effective contract-making, it pays to take account of the *context* of the contract.

What do I mean by the 'context' of a contract? I mean that you and your client can usefully consider the following three questions, and agree answers to them:

1   *Where* will the contract be carried out?
2   *When?*
3   Under what *limiting conditions?*

Each of these questions implies several other questions in turn. I shall discuss these more fully below.

Until now, TA writers on contract-making have paid little attention to the question of setting the context of an agreed contract. This contrasts with the situation in, for example, NLP, where the setting of a context is an essential part of working out a 'well-formed outcome' (see e.g. Andreas and Andreas 1989: 244–5).

It may seem at first sight as though the issue of context is dealt with in TA by the traditional demand that contracts should be 'behavioural and observable'. On closer inspection, however, it turns out that this is not necessarily so.

Take, for example, a simple behavioural contract like this one: 'In the coming week, I will say hello to three people I haven't spoken to before.' This statement is both sensory-based and finishable (recall Points 11 and 12). In other words, it is 'behavioural and observable' in traditional TA terms. However, the contract statement as it stands misses out part of the context. The *time* dimension of the contract is indeed specified ('in the coming week'). This answers the question 'when?'. But the dimension of 'where' is left unclear. Will the client say hello to three people on the upper deck of the bus, in the supermarket, at home, or just to three people anywhere?

Further, we do not know from the contract statement whether there are any circumstances in which the client would *not* carry out the contract. These are what I call 'limiting conditions'. For example, if the client is a woman, is she going to 'say hello to a new person' if that person is an unknown man she happens to pass in a deserted city street? If a man, is he going to 'say hello to three new people' in the Gents' toilet?

Why it is useful to specify the context of a contract

Why should it be useful to specify the context of a contract? Here are three reasons.

First and most importantly, it is a fact that every contract statement must *presuppose* a context. That is to say, all actions must take place in a context of some kind. Therefore, when you and your client are working out a contract, you have only two choices: you can either discuss and specify the context, or you can leave it unspecified. If you do leave it unspecified, you risk the possibility that you may actually be talking about different things when you think you are talking about the same thing. Thus, the central contractual principle of *mutual consent* may not be satisfied, though both you and the client may think it has been satisfied.

Second, the detail of the context may greatly affect the significance of the contract that you agree upon. It may even determine whether or not the agreed contract will further the client's script or help her to move out of it.

To give one example – suppose someone has come to counselling bringing the problems of overworking and difficulty in relating warmly to others. In script analysis you have found, not surprisingly, a Be Perfect driver message in the counterscript, and a Don't Be Close injunction in the script proper.

Suppose next that you and this client agree on her taking a contract: 'I will greet people in my workplace with a smile when I meet them.' At first sight, this may seem an appropriate contract for a behavioural movement out of script for the client.

This contract statement, however, leaves unspecified at least two questions about context. They are: 'Under what conditions?', and 'How often?'. Suppose that, when you raise these questions for discussion, the client reveals that, in her mind, the contract would apply to *everyone* and *at all times*. This carries the likelihood of reinforcing her Be Perfect counterscript belief. At the level of the script proper, the notion of 'smiling at everyone' could be seen as a counterphobic response to the client's Don't Be Close injunction. This would raise obvious concerns about protection.

Third, by specifying the context of a contract, you and your client give yourselves scope for 'fine-tuning' the statement of the contract itself. For example, in discussing the context of an overall contract to 'get close to others', the client may discover there are certain people she does *not* want to be close to, while there are others she does. All these realisations have the potential to be a useful part of the work of change. They allow the client to be more exact in describing the contract she wants to fulfil.

How closely does the context of a contract need to be specified?

You may be asking yourself: 'Does the contract, then, need to be given a fully specified context on each occasion of contract-making?'

My answer to that is no, but it is always a good idea to *enquire about and discuss the context* with your client. Your objective is to establish how far she wishes to make the context specific. You can then review her wish in the light of possible script implications.

To explain: there may be some occasions on which the client will wish deliberately to leave the context unspecified, in whole or in part. For example, let us return to the client who wants an overall contract to 'get close to others'. (Of course, at some stage in the process, you will discover what 'getting close' means to this client; that is not part of the issue in this discussion of context.) Suppose you ask her the specifying question: 'Where are you going to do this? Everywhere you go?' The client may possibly choose to leave the *place* aspect of context unspecified, perhaps saying that she does not want to limit herself at this stage to any particular place for carrying out the contracted action.

If so, your next check question for yourself and for her is: 'To what extent could you possibly be leaving a scripty cop-out from the contract by leaving this part of the context unspecified?'

In this case, it seems at least possible that the client in Child may be leaving a loophole that says: 'I won't, after all, get close to *these* people in the way I say in my contract, because I've just decided to call this place the wrong place.'

On the other side of the picture, it may be that the person is making a deliberate choice from Adult to leave the context somewhat open. If so, the open context gives the person more flexibility, hence more genuine Adult option, in where to choose to carry out the contracted action.

Questions to facilitate putting the contract in context

What are some practical ways of keeping the contract in context? The first and most important recommendation is that you keep the context in mind as you carry through the contract-making process with your client. Here are some questions that you can ask to elicit the three basic modalities of context: place, time and limiting conditions.

Where will the contract be carried out?

Where is the client going to do the action contracted for? Is it in some specific setting, for example, at her work, in her home? (A check question here is: 'What is the place by name?') Or is it to be in a generic setting, for example, whenever on top of a bus, or at some time when on the street? Or is the contract to apply anywhere and everywhere?

When?

You can investigate the time dimension of context by asking the client questions such as:

- by what date?
- how many weeks, months, years from now?
- how often?
- how many times?
- for how long once you have begun?

An important aim is to elicit from the client a statement of how long (or how often) the contract statement will need to be put into action for the client to be willing to say 'Yes, that contract is completed now.' Does she just need to do it once? If several times, how many times? If the focus is on achieving an end-point in a process (such as in a contract for reducing bodyfat), for how long does the target situation need to be held in place before the client will count the contract goal as having been achieved?

Under what limiting conditions?

The 'limiting conditions', of course, are already partly defined by 'where' and 'when'. Also, you will have begun to specify limiting conditions as you worked out with your client *whom specifically* she is going to carry out the contract with. Will the client carry out the contract when she is with one specific person or one specific group of people, for example, when she is with her children, or when she is with the five people who currently work in the office with her? (Again a check question here is, 'With whom by name?') Or is the contract to be completed with a generically defined group, for example, whenever with any workmates, or whenever she is with any people she has not met before? Or does the client specifically intend carrying out the contract with anyone and everyone?

Additional questions that may be useful are:

- 'What does the other person have to do first?'
- 'How will you know that it's time for you to do this?'
- 'Are there any circumstances in which you're *not* going to do this?'

Beware the 'invisible context'

It is as well to be cautious of agreeing statements of context such as the following:

- 'I'll show my feelings *when it's appropriate to show them.*'
- 'I'll express anger to my partner *when I feel angry.*'

The common feature of statements like these is that they specify a contextual circumstance that refers only to the client's own *internal* experience, and not to anything externally observable. I call this an 'invisible context'.

These 'invisible context' statements seem, and sometimes are, expressions of Adult caution. But in my experience, they are more often Child cop-outs. In Child, the person is defending against script change. He will likely discover that the occasion never seems to come when it is 'appropriate' to show his feelings, or that he seems inexplicably to have stopped 'feeling angry' just when he was on the point of expressing anger.

Useful check questions to pick up this kind of 'invisible context' are:

- 'If I were a fly on the wall, how would I know that the time had come when it was "appropriate" for you to show how you feel?'
- 'Are you willing to show your anger even if you don't believe you feel it?'

Key point

Be aware of the *context* of the contract. Consider with your client the following questions:

- where?
- when?
- under what limiting circumstances?

---

16 Bring the contract alive through visualisation

In this Point I describe a *contract visualisation* exercise. In it, you invite your client to imagine a scene in which he *has already got* the contractual change he desires. The client, literally, 'brings the contract goal alive' in his mind.

In Point 11, I mentioned that one benefit of a sensory-based contract was that it involved both you and your client in a positive visualisation of the contract outcome. The contract visualisation exercise is a logical extension of this idea.

The meaning of 'visualisation'

Though this activity is usually known as 'visualisation', it does not only entail 'seeing' in imagination. An essential aim of the exercise is to build up an internal representation of a desired scene, using not only seeing but also hearing and feeling (plus, sometimes, smelling and tasting as well). This may remind you of the criteria for a sensory-based contract (Point 11). The similarity is no accident.

Preparing for the visualisation

You will, as usual, begin by inviting a contract. Thus you will ask your client if he is willing to engage in an exercise where he simply relaxes and imagines himself having achieved what he wants to achieve. If you get an Adult 'Yes', you are working contractually, and the exercise can go on.

First see that the client is in a position where he can stay comfortable for the duration of the exercise. This will be about 15 minutes or so. Invite him to loosen tight clothing (tie, etc.) and remove shoes, insofar as he is comfortable to do so. If he is dubious about the prospect of 'going into a trance', you can reassure him that this is simply a process of relaxation, and that in fact everybody goes into some degree of trance many times every day, in the course of their normal activities.

If you already have your own favourite sequence for inviting relaxation or light trance, then use it at this point. Otherwise, simply invite the client to get comfortable and close his eyes; allow himself to hear the sounds around him; feel himself supported by the chair; be aware of his own breathing. At this point, the client should be relaxed enough to begin the visualisation.

Before starting the visualisation itself, you may find it useful to suggest to your client that he will stay awake enough to continue to hear your voice and be aware of what you are asking him to do. Also, he will remember the visualisation after he has completed it.

The contract visualisation exercise

The main objective of the exercise is to invite the client to construct an internal representation of the desired outcome that is as
rich as possible in sensory detail. The underlying pattern of the
sequence is simple:

1   You invite the client to *see* elements of the scene.
2   Then you invite him to *hear* sounds in the scene.
3   Next you invite him to *feel* sensations and emotions attached
    to the scene.

You may also ask him to bring smells and tastes into the scene if
he finds these are important.

Depending on the time available, you may invite the client to
cycle through these three stages several times, each time building
a more sensory-rich representation. It is important that you
yourself provide no content. You simply lead the client through
the different sensory systems – seeing, hearing, feeling, and
perhaps also smelling and tasting – and leave the client himself to
fill in his own sensory impressions.

You should keep stressing to the client that the scene he is
constructing in imagination is *his own*. He can remodel it at any
stage so that it becomes even more satisfying for him. However,
you should also remind the client that the scene has to be one
that is *possible in the real world*; no 'magic' is allowed.

You will notice how you use *verb tenses*. As you take the client
through the visualisation, use the *present* or *perfect* tenses (e.g.
'what you *are seeing*', 'the goal you *have achieved*'). Avoid the
future tense (e.g. 'the outcome you *will get*'). (I shall say more
about using verb tenses in Point 28.)

I suggest that you do not attempt to read from a written text,
nor to memorise a verbatim set of words. Instead, get the 'feel' of
the wording from my example, then improvise.

The kind of wording you might use is as follows, starting from
a point where the client is already well relaxed. As you speak, it
is a good idea to match your breathing with the client's. As he
breathes out, you speak. As he breathes in, you breathe in with
him. This matching does not need to be exact. In the wording
that follows, I have marked typical breathing pauses with three
dots.

'So now, as you continue to sit in your chair and hear my voice
as I talk to you . . . you can begin to let yourself imagine the

scene where you *have already* completely sorted out the problem that you brought to me here . . . and you can realise with pleasure that, in this scene you're imagining, you *have already got* whatever you needed to get, to make things really OK for you . . .

'And as you continue to take pleasure in realising this, you can let yourself be aware of what you *see* in this scene, when you have already got everything that you wanted to get . . .

'Maybe the scene is in some place you already know well . . . or maybe it's in a place that is new to you . . . whatever place it's in, is the right place for it to be in . . . and you can let yourself see more details of this place now . . .

'It may be that there is someone with you, or perhaps several people are with you . . . if there is anyone with you, who is that? Maybe you know them by name, or maybe they are new to you . . . you can simply be aware of who is with you in this scene, if anyone is with you . . . in this scene, where you *have already* sorted out everything that you wanted to sort out . . .

'And if there's any way you want to *change* what you're seeing, to let yourself know even more clearly that you've got what you wanted, then simply change what you see . . . this is your scene, so you can change it as you like. Your only limit is, keep to what's physically possible in the real world . . .

'And as you continue to see this scene, you can let yourself be aware now of what you *hear* . . . maybe you're saying something . . . maybe another person is saying something . . . and if anyone is speaking in this scene, let yourself hear what they're saying . . . and let yourself hear how they're saying it . . .

'And maybe there are other sounds in this scene . . . whatever sounds there are, simply let yourself go on hearing them . . .

'Notice just how you can *hear*, from the voices or whatever other sounds there are in this scene, that you *have already* got what you wanted . . .

'And if there's any way in which you can change what you're hearing, to let yourself know even more clearly that you've got what you wanted in this scene, go ahead and change it now . . . this is your scene, and you can have any sounds in it you want . . . just as long as you keep within what's possible in the real world . . .

'And as you go on hearing what you can hear, and seeing what you can see, now let yourself *feel* the feelings that go with this scene . . . the scene where you know clearly that you have got what you wanted . . .

'Maybe these feelings are physical feelings . . . like coolness, warmth, relaxation . . . or perhaps like the feel of some kind of clothing on your skin . . .

'And whether or not you're feeling any physical sensation, maybe you're feeling some kind of emotion . . . so simply allow yourself to feel that emotion now . . . maybe you're feeling happy, or satisfied, or fascinated . . . whatever feeling lets you know clearly that you have already sorted out what you wanted to sort out . . .

'And if there's any way that you want to change the sensations or the emotions you're feeling in this scene . . . to make the scene even more satisfying for you . . . go ahead and change those feelings now . . . it's your scene, and you can change it any way you want as long as you keep it in the bounds of reality . . .'

At this point, you have led the client through one round of seeing, hearing and feeling. As I have said, you can also give the client the option of adding anything he smells or tastes in the scene. Depending on what time is available, you can lead him through the entire sequence again, this time inviting him to be even more aware of the detail of what he sees, hears and feels. As before, invite him to make any desired changes to the scene, limited only by what is possible in the real world.

When you have taken the client through at most three cycles of the sequence, suggest once again that he will bring back from the visualisation a memory of what he has seen, heard and felt, and will be able to share the details of these experiences with you insofar as he wishes to.

Then raise the pitch and increase the pace of your voice. Invite the client to 'come back to the room, here at . . . [place] on . . . [date]'. When he opens his eyes, ask him to look round the room, find one thing he specially notices, and describe it to you. This completes the exercise.

The benefits of contract visualisation

There are several reasons why visualisation is a useful aid in contract-making. First, the exercise is a concrete, detailed application of the principle that when you make a contract *sensory-based*, you create a 'mental set' towards achieving that contract. In some way that we do not yet fully understand, a sensory-rich visualisation serves to orient the person's unconscious mind to the achievement of the contract goal.

Second, the process of visualisation is a test of the sensory-specificity of the stated contract. If the client *can* visualise a scene that is complete in all the details of what he is seeing, hearing and feeling, then this scene is, by definition, fully sensory-specific.

Third, often, visualisation helps the client arrive at a sensory-specific *marker* for a broader overall contract for script change (recall Point 13). You can ask the client to start the visualisation session simply with a statement of his broader contract goal, which will probably not be sensory-specific. Then you ask him to go ahead and fill in the sensory detail in the visualisation. If he succeeds in filling in all the detail, then he has arrived at one marker for the overall script-change contract.

Fourth, the visualisation also helps you and the client to learn and agree about the *context* of the contract (recall Point 15). Does the client report that he sees himself achieving the contract in a specific named place, with named people? Or is the background hazy and generalised, the people unknown faces? In the former case, this would be a highly specified context; in the latter, the context would be broad. Either is potentially OK, but they can have different implications for the script meaning of the contract. They may also affect the question of how you and the client will know when the contract has been completed.

Finally, what if the client reports that he has *not* achieved full detail in the visualisation? This sometimes does happen. For example, the client may not be able to see a part of the picture, or only be able to see it indistinctly. He may report not having experienced any sensations. These gaps in the visualisation can serve a useful diagnostic purpose. In my experience, they *always* alert both you and your client to areas of the script that the client still needs to attend to. If the client cannot see something, for example, this means that if he did see it, his scripty frame of reference would be threatened.

Thus, if the client reports incomplete areas in the visualisation, it is always a good idea to follow these up before proceeding any further with the contract-making. Sometimes a straightforward Adult question will be enough to help the client bring the script issue into awareness – for example, 'I wonder what you might be guarding against by not letting yourself see that part of the picture?'

Alternatively, a sentence completion may bring out Child material. You can offer the client an unfinished sentence like: 'I'm not letting myself feel any feelings in this scene, because I'm scared that if I *did* feel them, then . . .?' and ask him to finish the sentence in at least five different ways.

Key point

Visualisation allows the client to 'bring the contract alive' in his mind. You can use the visualisation exercise I have described in this Point.

Though the exercise is called 'visualisation', you ask the client to make a sensory-rich representation of what he can hear and feel (and perhaps smell and taste) as well as what he can see.

Using the Process Model

The Process Model is a framework for assessing personality and planning effective intervention. It is primarily the work of one man, Taibi Kahler (1974, 1978, 1979a, 1979b). Another TA innovator, Paul Ware (1983), originated the diagnostic system of six *personality adaptations* that now interacts with Kahler's ideas to make up the complete Process Model.

Kahler and Ware have been developing this material from the mid-1970s onwards. I believe it forms one of the most useful contributions that current TA has to offer you in the practice of counselling. You can readily use this set of techniques even if TA is not your main counselling approach.

The central skill of Process Model diagnosis is the detection of *driver behaviours* (Point 17). Knowing someone's driver pattern, you can go directly to a reliable judgement of her main *personality adaptation* (Point 19). This allows you to key in directly to a wealth of other information about the person's script and the ways in which you can best plan the course of counselling with her. All these features are described in the other Points of this section.

17 Be a skilled 'driver detective'

The skill of recognising *driver behaviours* is central to effective use of the Process Model (Kahler 1979a, 1979b). In this Point I describe the five different 'behaviour packages' that define the drivers, and give you practical recommendations on how to detect them.

Drivers are 'behaviour packages'

You will recall from Part I.e the names that Taibi Kahler used to label the five driver behaviours. They are:

- Be Perfect;
- Be Strong;
- Try Hard;
- Please You;
- Hurry Up.

Each of these names is a label for a specific set of *behaviours*. The person shows these behaviours over a very short time-period, typically no more than half-a-second at a time. It is by observing these behaviours, from one split second to the next, that you can reliably diagnose the different drivers.

Each of these 'behaviour packages' is made up of: *words, tones, gestures, postures* and *facial expressions*. The sets of these behaviours that define each driver are given in Table 17.1.

From my experience of working with the Process Model, I have made two minor changes to the table of driver clues originally given by Kahler (1979b). First, I have added a few behaviours that Kahler did not list. I believe these are reliable clues to particular drivers. (I stress that I have made these additions on the evidence of *observation* – that is, because I have so often seen people exhibiting the behaviours in question along with the other clues to that particular driver. I have *not* added them because I somehow think the behaviours 'should' fit into these particular drivers.) I have marked these added clues on Table 17.1 with an asterisk.

My second amendment is to emphasise some behaviours that, in my experience, are most highly diagnostic of the driver in question. These behaviours I have shown in bold type on Table 17.1.

Detecting driver behaviour

Here are three points of guidance to keep in mind when you are looking out for driver behaviours:

1 Get used to observing within split seconds.
2 Look for clusters of behavioural clues.
3 Pick out the person's primary driver(s).

Get used to observing within split seconds

The first practical 'how-to' on driver detection is this: you need to get accustomed to using an observation span that counts its time

Table 17.1 *Behavioural clues to drivers*

Driver	Words	Tones	Gestures	Postures	Facial expressions
Be Perfect	**Phrases in parentheses** Counts points off by numbers 'As it were' 'As we have seen' 'That is to say'	Clipped Even Well-modulated Precise enunciation	Counts on fingers Strokes chin 'Steeples' fingertips (V-shape)*	Upright Balanced round midline (resembles Adult)	Eyes look upwards (less often downwards) and to **one side, during pauses*** Mouth slightly tensed, pulled out at corners*
Be Strong	('Distancing', e.g.:) **'You make me angry'** **'This bores me'** **'It feels good'**	Flat Monotonous Usually low	**Gestures few or absent**	**Immobile** Closed (arms folded, legs crossed)	**Immobile** Expressionless
Try Hard	'I'll try to . . .' 'I can't' 'It's difficult' **'Huh? Uh? What?'** 'Don't get you'	Muffled **Tense Strangled** Hesitant	**Hand by side of head (as if straining to see or hear)*** Clenched fists	Strains forward Hunched-up	Screws up brow (two vertical lines above nose)
Please You	**'(High) . . . *but* . . . (low)'** 'OK? All right?' 'Kind of, sort of' 'Hmmm?'	High Squeaky **Rises at end of sentence**	Head nodding Hands reaching out (usually palms up)	**Shoulders hunched up and forward** Leans towards other person	Turns face downward Looks up under raised eyebrows Crinkles brow into horizontal lines Exaggerated smile, teeth bared
Hurry Up	**'Quick'** 'Must rush' 'Let's go' 'No time'	Staccato Machine-gun-like Runs words together Fidgets	**Taps fingers Wags foot** Wriggles	Agitated changes of posture	Rapid, frequent shifts in gaze

Source: Kahler (1979b and workshop presentations). Modifications by the present author are indicated by bold type and asterisks (see text).

units in half- and quarter-seconds, rather than in minutes, hours or counselling sessions.

For example, consider this exchange:

> *Counsellor*: So will you tell me what you want to get from our session today?
> *Client*: Umm . . . [*She looks up and to the right, while moving the corners of her mouth outwards very slightly and placing her fingertips together in front of her chest.*] Well! [*Her voice moves to higher pitch, rising at the end of the syllable. At the same time she raises her eyebrows so that horizontal wrinkles appear on her forehead, while opening her eyes wide, opening her mouth so as to reveal her upper teeth, and leaning towards the counsellor, extending her hands towards him palms-up.*]

That description took much longer for you to read than it took to happen. The client showed all these behaviours, in real time, within just over one second. During that time, she exhibited first the Be Perfect, then the Please You drivers.

Given that you are willing to make this shift to a very short time frame, you will find driver behaviours easy to detect. It does take a certain amount of practice to get used to the second-by-second observation that is needed. However, in detecting drivers you are not called upon to pick up subtle micro-behaviours. Drivers are defined by readily observable, *fast* macro-behaviours.

Look for clusters of behavioural clues

Taibi Kahler stresses: 'No one behavioural clue necessitates a driver' (Kahler 1979b: 20). For reliable driver detection, you need to look and listen for a *cluster* of clues, drawn from all five areas of the person's behaviour: words, tones, gestures, postures and facial expressions. I would suggest in practice that you only diagnose the driver when you observe at least three clues to that driver being shown *together*.

Pick out the primary driver(s)

When you are using driver detection to help you diagnose other aspects of script – that is, to key into the Process Model – then it is important to judge what is the person's *primary driver*. This is the driver they show most frequently in a sample of conversation. It will most often also be the driver they show *first* as they respond to your communication.

People typically show driver behaviours at frequent intervals in every interaction. In any sample of conversation lasting two minutes, you will usually have seen and heard more than enough driver clues to make a judgement about the person's primary driver.

It is irrelevant *what* you and the client talk about during that time. You are observing process (the 'how'), not content (the 'what').

It is a good idea to pay special attention to the *pause* that may often occur after you have said something to the client or asked him a question. It is during that pause that the person will often show his or her primary driver.

Most people show one of the five driver behaviours that is clearly their primary driver. A smaller group will show two drivers that are about first-equal in frequency; and an even smaller minority will exhibit three or more drivers that share first place.

In my experience, the Hurry Up driver is in many ways an 'odd man out' among the driver behaviours. You will seldom observe it as a primary driver. Instead, it most often occurs as a secondary driver and serves as a reinforcement to the primary driver.

Driver clues: some extra hints

Here are some additional 'household hints' on detecting drivers. First, as you observe your client from second to second, you will also notice her showing many other behavioural clues that are *not* part of any driver behaviour. However, you will soon develop the skill of separating out the five distinctive 'bundles' of clues that consistently occur together to signal the driver behaviours.

Second, the use of *words in parentheses* is a particularly telling clue to the Be Perfect driver. The effect of the parentheses is to put in one or more pieces of qualifying information before the speaker lets himself get to the end of the sentence. Some examples are:

- 'My intention – as I was saying in the meeting today, and as I have made clear on numerous occasions before now – is to take action about this situation.'
- 'This book is, you might say, a brief guide to TA.'

Third, though the phrase 'I'll try . . .' is often associated with the Try Hard driver, it is *not* in itself diagnostic of that driver.

Before judging whether 'I'll try . . .' indicates Try Hard, you need to check supplementary clues from tones, gestures, and so on.

And fourth, the person showing the Please You driver often uses a 'high – (but) – low' sentence pattern. The sentence begins with an excited reference to something the person finds good. Then there is a fulcrum, often represented by the word 'but'. The sentence concludes with a 'low', referring to something unpleasant for the person. Some examples are:

- 'Hey, I'm really enjoying this party! But, oh dear, what a head I'm going to have in the morning.'
- 'I thought your teaching was great! But I'm not sure if I've really understood you.'

Caution: you cannot detect drivers by observing content

To detect drivers effectively, you must focus on *process*. You cannot detect drivers by observing the *content* of the person's behaviour.

For example, suppose you notice that someone 'wants to do things perfectly'. That may be of interest to you in itself. But it is *not* diagnostic of the Be Perfect driver. 'Wanting to get things perfect' has to do with the content of the person's behaviour, not its process. If you did want to know whether this person showed the Be Perfect driver, you would check from second to second whether he often used parentheses in his speech patterns, looked upwards during pauses, or counted out points with his fingers.

Likewise, suppose another person answers 'Yes' when asked in a questionnaire: 'Do you find it important to please others?' Again, this tells you something about her personality. But it is *not* a way to diagnose the Please You driver. That driver, like all the others, consists in a package of quite specific, short-lived behaviours. To detect Please You, you would not look for general 'pleasingness'. You would check whether the person momentarily raised her eyebrows, bared her upper teeth, turned her face down while looking upwards, hunched her shoulders around her ears, and said *anything* in a high and rising voice tone.

Both within TA and outside it, some writers have put together entire books starting from the mistaken notion that you could detect drivers from content. Learned academics have devoted time and resources to questionnaire studies based upon the same misapprehension. In reality, the books are mere fairy-stories, and the questionnaire results are not worth the journal paper they are written on. In your practical work of counselling, you know now not to make the same mistake.

Driver behaviour is a 'gateway into script'

In the coming Points in this section, I shall describe how driver detection allows you to key into the other diagnostic features of the Process Model. However, even without this advantage, driver observation would be useful in itself. This is because driver behaviours are a 'gateway into script'. You can either use this fact diagnostically, or move immediately to confront the script belief in question.

One of Kahler's earliest discoveries about driver behaviours was that, just before a person experiences a racket feeling or internally 'hears' an injunction, she will *always* show driver behaviour (Kahler 1974). It is as though the person moving into script must unavoidably do so by going through a driver 'gateway'.

The significance of this for you is clear. There are many situations where it is useful for you to know whether a particular item of behaviour, or a particular reported feeling, is scripty or is not scripty. For example, suppose the client laughs. Is this a gallows laugh or an autonomous laugh? Or suppose she expresses anger. Is this racket or authentic anger?

Here is the clue that driver behaviour gives you: did the client engage in driver behaviour *just before* she laughed, or just before she expressed the feeling? If the answer is 'no', then you know that the client has *not* moved into script.

Note, however, that the reasoning does not necessarily work in the converse direction. As I have said, the person who goes into script will always show driver behaviour just before doing so. But it is also possible for the person to show a driver behaviour and then *not* go into script. She may, instead, simply move back out of the driver behaviour into non-scripty feelings and behaviours. So, in summary:

1 If *no* driver behaviour: subsequent feeling or behaviour is *not* scripty.
2 If driver behaviour: subsequent feeling or behaviour *may or may not* be scripty.

Table 17.2   *Counterscript beliefs underlying driver behaviours*

Driver	Counterscript belief
Be Perfect	I'm only OK if I get everything right (therefore, I've got to cover every detail before I can finish anything)
Be Strong	I'm only OK if I disown my feelings and wants
Try Hard	I'm only OK if I keep on trying hard (therefore, I won't actually do what I'm trying to do; because if I did it, I wouldn't be 'trying to' do it any more)
Please You	I'm only OK if I please other people
Hurry Up	I'm only OK if I hurry up

Source: compiled by present author from Kahler (1974, 1978).

Driver behaviour is itself an expression of counterscript

As well as being the 'gateway' through which the person may move further into script, driver behaviour itself indicates that the person is already replaying one of her script beliefs internally (Kahler 1974). All these script beliefs are part of the *counterscript* (recall Part I.d). Each has the form: 'I'm OK *as long as I . . .*'.

In Table 17.2, I list the counterscript slogan that follows this phrase for each of the five drivers.

If you wish, when you observe your client showing a driver behaviour, you can immediately confront the content of the matching counterscript belief. Here are examples:

> Client: [*looks upwards and to one side, counts on fingers*] What I'd like to do, as I said before, is tell you exactly what I want from this session.
> Counsellor: Would it be OK by you to start by telling me approximately what you want? [*Confronts Be Perfect script belief.*]

> Client: [*hunches forwards, screws brow into two vertical lines, strangled voice tone*] Ahh, well . . . what we're talking about seems difficult to me, but . . . hmm . . . I'll give it a try.
> Counsellor: Well, yeah, 'giving it a try' would be one thing you could do. Alternatively, you could just go ahead and *do* it. How does that grab you? [*Confronts Try Hard script belief.*]

In Points 21 and 22, I shall say more about how you can use *contact areas* and *communication Channels* to fine-tune your interventions in response to the different driver behaviours.

> **Key point**
>
> Look and listen, second by second, for the distinctive 'behaviour packages' that define the five driver behaviours.
>
> Notice how driver behaviour is a 'gateway into script'.
>
> You can use your driver observations diagnostically by keying into other information in the Process Model (see the coming Points). You may also directly confront the counterscript belief that underlies that driver behaviour.

18   Avoid inviting drivers

If you show a driver behaviour while communicating with your client, the chances are that she will respond to you with another driver behaviour. This may either be her own primary driver or a return of whatever driver you have shown. As Taibi Kahler says, 'Driver invites driver' (1979b).

Therefore it is important that you stay out of driver behaviour as much as possible while you are counselling. In this Point I suggest ways in which you can achieve this.

Driver behaviour is an invitation into counterscript

Why does 'driver invite driver'? We get an answer by considering the script implications of drivers (recall Point 17 and Part I.e). Every time I show a driver behaviour externally, I am internally replaying one of my counterscript beliefs.

For example, in the course of a counselling session I may get into the Be Perfect driver behaviour. As I do so, I am internally stating my counterscript belief: 'I've got to cover the entire waterfront before I can finish anything around here.'

Outside of his awareness, my client notes my driver behaviour. He picks up my script belief at the psychological level. He is then likely to say to *himself*, out of awareness: 'To be OK around here, people have to . . . get things Perfect' (or, perhaps, 'Try Hard', or 'Please Others', or whatever message he most often heard in his own childhood). In other words, he internally states his own counterscript belief. And, externally, he signals this by showing one of the driver behaviours.

This is why, each time you show a driver behaviour, you are inviting your client into his own counterscript. Clearly, this is an outcome you want to avoid as much as possible. Any time you issue a script invitation to your client, you are inadvertently sabotaging the aims of counselling.

In particular, when you are using driver observation to help you in diagnosis, you may obscure accurate assessment if you show driver behaviour yourself. In that case, some of the client's driver behaviour is likely to be simply a reflection of your own driver behaviour.

The importance of personal work for the counsellor

Since driver behaviours are an expression of script, it follows that you can lower the intensity and frequency of your drivers by becoming more free from your script – by engaging in personal counselling or psychotherapy. This, of course, is necessary in any case for you as a practitioner.

However, Taibi Kahler asserts that even the most script-free individuals still engage in driver behaviour for a large proportion of the time in normal conversation (Kahler, workshop presentation). Thus, says Kahler, personal counselling or therapy alone will not ensure that your communications as a practitioner will be driver-free. This being so, it is a good idea to take time deliberately to practise staying out of driver.

Nobody, not even the most experienced counsellor, succeeds in staying out of driver all the time. But it is a matter of playing the percentages – the more you succeed in staying out of driver, the more your client is likely to stay out with you.

Avoiding typical driver invitations in word patterns

As a contribution to staying out of driver, there are some common forms of words that you can usefully *avoid* during counselling. Here are some of the most common driver-laden wordings that counsellors may use, with the italicised words indicating the driver clues. After each example, I give a suggested driver-free translation.

1(a) 'Tell me what you want *specifically*.' (*Invites Be Perfect*)

1(b) (*Driver-free*:) 'Tell me what you want.'

2(a) 'How does that *make you feel?*' (*Invites Be Strong*)

2(b) (*Driver-free*:) 'How do you feel about that?'

3(a) 'What *thought comes to you*?' (*Invites Be Strong*)

3(b) (*Driver-free*:) 'What are you thinking?'

4(a) '*Can you / Could you* tell me what you mean?' (*Invites Try Hard*)

4(b) (*Driver-free*:) 'What do you mean?'

5(a) '*Try to* explain to me what you mean.' (*Invites Try Hard*)

5(b) (*Driver-free*:) 'Will you explain to me what you mean?'

6(a) 'Do you want to go on, *or do you want to stop?*' (*Asking two questions at once: invites Try Hard*)

6(b) (*Driver-free*:) 'You could go on now, or you could stop. Which do you want to do?'

7(a) '*I want you to / I'd like you to* express how you feel.' (*Invites Please You*)

7(b) (*Driver-free*:) 'If you want to express how you feel, please go ahead.'

Avoiding non-verbal driver signals

In order for *any* form of words to be genuinely driver-free, you also need to avoid making the other behavioural signals of the driver in question.

For example, suppose the counsellor used the driver-free wording in the last example above: 'If you want to express how you feel, please go ahead.' But suppose also, as she said this sentence, she did the following:

- used a voice pitch that was higher than her usual register, and that got even higher as she said the last few words;
- leaned towards the client;
- reached out her hands, palms up, towards the client in a 'gathering' gesture;
- looked upward at the client under raised eyebrows;
- 'smiled' so as to show her upper teeth.

She would, of course, be showing Please You by these behaviours. Thus she would be inviting a return of the Please You driver (or, less likely, another driver) from the client.

You will notice that this pictured set of behaviours is one that would often be described as 'warm' or 'accepting' in a counselling situation. (If you like, test this by role-playing it in front of a mirror.) This underlines the possibility that counsellors may *learn* some behaviours that have the potential to invite driver behaviour in the client. Some of these behaviours may even be taught or modelled in some counselling trainings.

This is true par excellence of the demeanour of the counsellor or psychotherapist who keeps a traditional 'poker face' and reveals little expression in his position, movement, gestures or voice tone. Outside of awareness, it is likely that the client will read such 'dead-pan' behaviour as an invitation into the Be Strong driver.

Self-supervision: detecting your own driver behaviours

Experience shows that people often find it difficult to assess their own primary driver, even when they are familiar with driver clues in others. Thus the *only* reliable way to make an initial assessment of your own driver behaviours is to have yourself observed by someone else who is familiar with driver clues.

If possible, have yourself and your client videotaped during a counselling session. You can also use an audiotaped session, though it is a second-best because you will only hear the audible clues to driver behaviours. Choose a segment of tape no more than five minutes in length.

Pay attention to word patterns and voice tones, and if on videotape to gestures, postures and facial expressions. Bear in mind that driver signals are typically shown within periods of less than one second. Pay particular attention to pauses. Referring to Table 17.1, note the following:

1 At what points did your client show driver behaviour? At each of these points, which driver did she show?
2 At what points did you show driver behaviour? Which driver?
3 Replay the tape to review driver interactions. When either you or the client showed a driver, did the other person respond by also showing a driver?
4 On the evidence of the tape, what do you judge to be your client's primary driver or principal drivers?

5 What do you judge to be your own primary driver or principal drivers?

6 Practise catching your driver behaviour before you show it. Instead, switch into communicating without driver signals. If possible, get further feedback by having more sessions videotaped.

Another useful method of practising avoiding drivers, especially if you cannot make videotapes of your sessions, is to find at least two other people to form a peer group. Within that group, take turns as counsellor and client, with the other or others acting as observers of driver clues. Each 'counselling' session need be no more than three minutes long. At the end of this period, the observer gives feedback on driver clues as in (1) to (5) above.

You can continue the exercise by having a further round of sessions, in which the counsellor practises staying out of driver. The observer feeds back at the end of each session what he saw and heard differently in the interaction between counsellor and client.

Using communication Channels

In this Point, I have framed your task as one of *avoiding* driver-laden communication. This is a useful skill in itself. However, the Process Model allows you not only to *avoid* drivers in communication, but also actively to choose modes of communication that you can use to put something positive *in place of* drivers. You do so by using *communication Channels*. I shall describe them in Point 22.

Key point

Get used to picking up your own driver behaviours.

In counselling sessions, catch each driver behaviour just *before* you show it. Choose an alternative behaviour that is driver-free.

19 Recognise the six personality adaptations

Central to Process Model diagnosis is the assessment of *personality adaptations*. These represent six ways in which a person may deal with the world, particularly when under stress. In this Point I describe how you can recognise these six adaptations.

Why is it useful to know personality adaptation?

When you know your client's main personality adaptation, you can key in directly to a whole body of extra information that is likely to apply to that client. Each adaptation carries with it a typical set of *script beliefs* about self, others and the world. Along with these go typical emotions and patterns of behaviour that the person is likely to show while in script – that is, their *rackets* and *racket feelings*. This knowledge helps you decide on the treatment direction that will most effectively meet each client's needs.

Equally, each personality adaptation has typical positive traits that the person can use constructively. You can plan your treatment so that your client builds on these strengths.

By knowing someone's personality adaptation, you also gain guidance on how best to make and keep contact with that person. To do this, you make a systematic choice of the sequence in which you address the person's three *contact areas* of thinking, feeling or behaviour. This is the *Ware Sequence* (see Point 21). You can enhance rapport still further by choosing one of five *communication Channels*. This means deciding *how* you say whatever you say. Knowledge of personality adaptation helps you in this choice also (see Point 22).

The six personality adaptations

The concept of personality adaptations was developed by Paul Ware (1983). As part of the process of script-formation, says Ware, every child decides on a set of basic strategies for surviving and getting needs met. The person may sometimes replay these strategies in grown-up life, particularly in stress situations. They then represent various ways of *adapting to* the world. Ware distinguishes six main sets of these strategies. They correspond to his list of six personality adaptations.

All 'normal' people, says Ware, display all six adaptations to some degree. However, most of us have one adaptation that is dominant. Sometimes a person will show two adaptations more or less equally.

Ware's six personality adaptations correspond broadly to certain formal diagnostic categories. He labels them with names drawn from clinical psychodiagnosis. However, Ware stresses that his use of these labels does not necessarily imply psychopathology in a clinical sense. A person can show the characteristics of one or more of Ware's categories, while still being clinically 'normal'. A formal clinical diagnosis will only be attached if a person shows a particular adaptation at such high intensity as to disrupt his day-to-day functioning.

To underline this, I shall give an alternative set of names for the personality adaptations, suggested by Vann Joines (1986). I list these names below, each following the traditional diagnostic label that was applied to the adaptation by Paul Ware. (In place of Ware's original label 'Hysteric', I have used the term 'Histrionic' that is now more usual.)

- Obsessive-compulsive (Responsible Workaholic)
- Paranoid (Brilliant Sceptic)
- Schizoid (Creative Daydreamer)
- Passive-aggressive (Playful Critic)
- Histrionic (Enthusiastic Over-Reactor)
- Antisocial (Charming Manipulator).

By the adjective he adds to each name, Joines underlines the important point that each adaptation has its advantages as well as its problems.

If you are used to making traditional psychodiagnoses, you can apply the Ware scheme to 'normal' clients simply by noting the same traits as you would assess for a clinical diagnosis. However, you would expect these traits to be shown at a lower intensity than in clients who would merit the clinical diagnostic label. Table 19.1 lists the personality traits that define each personality adaptation (Ware 1983; Joines 1986).

Table 19.1   *Features defining personality adaptations*

Adaptation	Characteristics	Description
Workaholic (*Obsessive-compulsive*)	Conformity Conscientiousness Responsibility Reliability	Perfectionist Inhibited Conscientious Dutiful Tense Dependable Organised Neat
Sceptic (*Paranoid*)	Rigidity of thought Grandiosity Projection Clarity of thought Alertness Attention to detail	Hypersensitive Suspicious Jealous Envious Knowledgeable Careful
Daydreamer (*Schizoid*)	Withdrawn passivity Daydreaming Avoidance Detachment Artistic ability Creative thinking Concern for others	Shy Sensitive Eccentric Caring Supportive Pleasant Kind
Critic (*Passive-aggressive*)	Aggressive passivity Resentment Over-dependence Determination to think for herself Weighs both sides of an issue	Obstructive Stubborn Petulant Loyal Energetic Engaging Fun-loving Tenacious
Over-Reactor (*Histrionic*)	Excitability Emotional instability Over-reactivity Dramatic behaviour Attention-seeking Seductiveness High in energy Concerned about others' feelings Imaginative	Immature Self-centred Vain Dependent Playful Attractive Fun to be with
Manipulator (*Antisocial*)	Conflict with society Low frustration tolerance Need for excitement and drama High energy Goal-orientation Thinks well on his feet	Selfishness Callousness Irresponsibility Impulsiveness Charm Charisma Aggressiveness Articulateness Manipulation

Source: Ware (1983) with additions by Joines (1986).

Self-supervision: assessing personality adaptation from qualitative evidence

Consider one client you are working with. Refer to Table 19.1. On the evidence of your acquaintance with her so far, make an initial judgement of this client's main personality adaptation or adaptations. Simply check through the qualitative traits shown in the table and see how far your client's 'cluster' of traits fits the adaptation(s) listed.

How drivers indicate personality adaptations

You can go directly to a judgement of personality adaptation within a few minutes of first meeting the client, and without the need for traditional 'history-taking'. You do this by observing the client's driver behaviours.

By noting a person's *primary driver* (recall Point 17) you can make a reliable diagnosis of his main personality adaptation. Table 19.2 shows the correspondences between drivers and personality

Table 19.2   *Correspondences between primary drivers and personality adaptations*

Primary driver(s)	Personality adaptation
Be Perfect (Be Strong)	Workaholic
Be Perfect = Be Strong	Sceptic
Be Strong (Try Hard or Please You)	Daydreamer
Try Hard (Be Strong)	Critic
Please You (Try Hard or Hurry Up)	Over-Reactor
Be Strong (Please You)	Manipulator

Note: Brackets indicate likely secondary drivers.

Source: Ware (1983) collated with Kahler (1979b).

adaptations. For each adaptation, the primary driver may often be accompanied by secondary drivers. These are shown in brackets. The Sceptic adaptation is marked by a combination of Be Perfect and Be Strong driver signals, shown with about equal intensity.

Self-supervision: assessing personality adaptation from driver evidence

For the client you chose for the previous self-supervision, now review your qualitative assessment of her main personality adaptation. Compare it with your reading of her driver behaviours. Check these two sets of clues one against the other. Does the relationship between drivers and personality adaptation fit the correspondences shown in Table 19.2?

If not, review your assessment of both sets of clues. These correspondences between driver and adaptation are highly reliable. The most common reason for an apparent mismatch is that you have not correctly identified the client's primary driver.

Personality adaptation and script content

In the coming Points, I shall explain how you can use your knowledge of personality adaptation to key into other main diagnostic features of the Process Model, notably the person's *contact area* (Point 21) and *communication Channel* (Point 22). However, even without that important advantage, knowing the client's personality adaptation gives you immediate clues to various other features of her script. These are features of script *content* (the 'what'), not of script process (the 'how').

Each personality adaptation is accompanied by a 'cluster' of typical *script messages* and *racket feelings*. These, of course, are two of the main features you would be investigating if you were using a script questionnaire (recall Point 6). By knowing the person's main personality adaptation, you can develop a good initial picture of this script content. And you can reliably judge his or her personality adaptation, on the evidence of the primary driver, in the space of about two minutes' conversation. Further, as always with the Process Model, it does not matter *what* you talk about. You can be making your Process Model diagnosis, using the *process* of communication, even while the client is explaining to you the *content* of his presenting problem.

However, there is a need for caution here. The correspondence between personality adaptation and script beliefs and rackets is a matter of probability, not of certainty. In this respect, it differs from the link between drivers and personality adaptations. Adaptations match primary drivers exactly. For example, if I see clearly that somebody's primary driver is Be Perfect, then I *know for certain* that his main personality adaptation will be Workaholic. However, when I go on to predict his most important script messages and racket feelings, my knowledge of his primary adaptation only lets me do so approximately.

For example, I can read off from the tables that the Workaholic person's 'typical injunctions' include Don't Be Close. This lets me know that, for *this* Workaholic client, there is a good chance that the Don't Be Close injunction will indeed be prominent in his script. However, for a more reliable reading of the person's script, I will need to check this against longer-term observation of his own unique script content. These Process Model readings of script content are most useful in giving you an initial 'snapshot' of the script, which you can then go on to cross-check by means of a formal script analysis.

Of course, there will be times when you only have a small number of sessions in which to work with a particular client. In these cases, it is particularly helpful to be able to use the Process Model to give you a quick view of the person's most likely script content.

Keeping this qualification in mind, you can use Tables 19.3 and 19.4 to get a 'snapshot' of the person's most likely injunctions and racket feelings, using your knowledge of her main personality adaptation.

Reminder: drivers indicate counterscript beliefs

By now, as well as having a reliable guide to the person's probable injunctions and racket feelings, you also know something about the content of her counterscript. You will recall from Point 17 that the driver behaviours themselves indicate messages in the counterscript (Table 17.2). Thus your Process Model diagnosis has given you a serviceable initial picture of the *content* of the client's script.

Table 19.3 *Typical injunctions for different personality adaptations*

Adaptation	Typical injunctions
Workaholic (*Obsessive-compulsive*)	Don't Be a Child (Don't Enjoy) Don't Feel (joy, sexuality) Don't Be Close
Sceptic (*Paranoid*)	Don't Be a Child (Don't Enjoy) Don't Be Close Don't Feel Don't Belong
Daydreamer (*Schizoid*)	Don't Make It Don't Belong Don't Enjoy Don't Be Sane Don't Grow Up Don't Feel (joy, sexuality, love) Don't Think
Critic (*Passive-aggressive*)	Don't Grow Up Don't Feel Don't Enjoy Don't Be Close Don't Make It
Over-Reactor (*Histrionic*)	Don't Grow Up Don't Think Don't Be Important Don't Be the Sex You Are (in males)
Manipulator (*Antisocial*)	Don't Make It Don't Be Close Don't Feel (scare, sadness) Don't Think (in terms of future problem-solving; OK to think to outsmart or 'make fools of' people)

Note: The injunction 'Don't Exist' may be among the script messages for *any* of the six personality adaptations, appearing in addition to the other injunctions typical of the adaptation in question.

Source: Revised by Joines (1986) from Ware (1983).

Table 19.4   *Racket feelings typical of personality adaptations*

Adaptation	Racket feelings
Workaholic	Irritation Anxiety Depression Guilt covering anger Anger covering sadness
Sceptic	Jealousy Envy Suspicion Blamefulness Anger covering scare
Daydreamer	Anxiety ⎫ Worry ⎬ covering anger, hurt Sadness ⎭ Confusion (blankness)
Critic	Righteous indignation Confusion covering anger at others Frustration covering hurt
Over-Reactor	Scare ⎫ Sadness ⎬ covering anger Confusion ⎭ Anger covering scare or sadness
Manipulator	Blamelessness Confusion Anger covering scare or sadness

Source: Collated by the present author from Kahler (1979b), Ware (1983) and Joines (1986).

Self-supervision: script beliefs and personality adaptation

Review the assessment you have already made of your client's driver behaviours and personality adaptation.

1 Consulting Table 17.2, note the counterscript belief that corresponds to your client's primary driver.
2 From Table 19.3, note the script messages given as being typical of the client's main personality adaptation.

3 If you have not yet done a formal script analysis (Point 6) with this client, do one now. Cross-check the resulting list of script messages and beliefs against the list you have made on the evidence of her drivers and personality adaptation. How well do the two lists agree?

4 Consider the points on which the two lists agree and those on which they differ, and draw up a consolidated list. You may also wish to review your assessment of the client's primary driver and personality adaptation.

Key point

Assess your clients' personality adaptation(s). Do this both by observing their personality features and by checking their driver behaviours.

You can use your knowledge of personality adaptation to key into further features of the Process Model, or to give you a 'snapshot' of the *content* of your client's script – or both.

---

20 Confront the process script

One of your main tasks in inviting script change is to stay aware of script process patterns, both your own and your client's. As well as confronting the *content* of your client's script, you can confront her script *process* in order to invite effective change. In this Point, I suggest ways in which you can do this.

Six process script types

You will recall from Part I.e that 'script process' means the 'how' of the script, while 'script content' means the 'what'. Script content says what there is in the person's script; script process says how she lives it out over time. Eric Berne (1972) described six different types of process script:

- Until
- Never
- Always
- After
- Almost
- Open-Ended.

Kahler (1978: 216–7) suggests that the Almost pattern can be subdivided into *Almost Type I* and *Almost Type II*. I shall follow his scheme here.

Each of the process script titles describes a pattern of *how* the person will live out her script over time. Each pattern can be summed up in a motto, which reflects the person's early decisions about self, others or the world. Table 20.1 gives the mottoes and patterns for the different process script types.

Process script and driver behaviour

Each process script pattern is directly associated with particular driver behaviours. Table 20.1 lists the correspondences between drivers and process scripts.

I described in Point 17 how you can detect driver behaviour and, in Point 19, how you can use it in diagnosing personality adaptation. Now you are able also to make a reliable assessment of process script type from the moment-to-moment observation of your client's driver behaviours.

You know that everyone shows all five drivers, but that most people have one primary driver. Correspondingly, everyone has traits of all six process scripts, but most people typically have one that predominates. That one is the process script type associated with their primary driver.

Three of the process patterns (Almost I, Almost II and Open-Ended) are typically observed in persons who have two drivers about equal. The specific driver combinations for these process scripts are shown in Table 20.1. Both the Almost II and the Open-Ended scripts are indicated by a combination of Please You and Be Perfect. However, the person with the Open-Ended script will show both drivers more intensely than the person who has an Almost II script.

Process scripts and personality adaptations

As an alternative to diagnosing process script type directly from driver behaviour, you can also go by your assessment of the

Table 20.1   *Characteristics of different process script types*

Name	Motto	Pattern	Driver(s)
Until	'I can't have fun until I've finished all my work'	Stops self from getting something pleasant until something unpleasant has been completed	Be Perfect
Never	'I never get what I most want'	Doesn't get started, doesn't get anywhere	Be Strong
Always	'I've made my bed, now I have to lie in it'	Stays with situations even when negative	Try Hard
After	'I can have fun today, but I'll have to pay for it tomorrow'	Gets something pleasant but then punishes self with something unpleasant	Please Others
Almost I	'I almost get to the top of the hill, but then slip all the way down again'	Gets started (on projects etc.) but doesn't quite finish	Please Others + Try Hard
Almost II	'I get to the top of the hill and immediately start off for an even higher hill'	Finishes (project etc.) and goes on without pausing to another task	Please You + Be Perfect
Open-Ended	'After a certain point in time, I won't know what to do with myself'	Reaches a certain point in life, in projects etc. and then 'hits a blank'	Please You + Be Perfect

Source: Compiled by present author from Kahler (1979b).

Table 20.2 *Process script types for different personality adaptations*

Personality adaptation	Process Script Type(s)
Workaholic	Until (Almost II, Dead End)
Sceptic	Until + Never
Daydreamer	Never (Always)
Critic	Always (Never, Almost I)
Over-Reactor	After (Almost I, Almost II)
Manipulator	Never (Always, Almost)

Note: Brackets indicate likely subsidiary process script types.

Source: Compiled by the present author from Kahler (1979b).

person's main personality adaptation. These correspondences are shown in Table 20.2. As you would expect, they give you the same results as diagnosing directly from the person's driver behaviours; this is just an alternative 'way round'.

Time-scale of the process script

When in script, the person will typically play out his process pattern over both short and long time-spans. He may run the whole process pattern within a few seconds. He may play it out over days, months, or years, and it will also constitute a plan for his entire life-script.

For example, suppose the person's principal process script is Until. You may find him at age 40 already planning for his retirement. In order to build up a big enough nest-egg for that future 'Until', he works so hard in the present that he doesn't have a great deal of time to enjoy life. Day by day, he is at his desk until six p.m. He comes home, deals with all his correspondence, and goes jogging before he is ready to relax for the evening. Then his friend calls to see if he wants to go out for a drink. He replies: 'OK, with you in a minute – just got to tidy up these papers first.'

Like other features of the script, process script patterns can be used positively as well as negatively. For instance, the man in our example uses his Until pattern to motivate himself to keep up a fitness programme. Only if the process pattern is producing unacceptable results for the person need it become the object of change in counselling.

Confronting the process script

In principle, confronting the client's process script is straightforward. You bring the pattern to her attention and ask if she will take a contract to behave differently. You can also stroke every behaviour that contravenes the process script pattern.

Caution

As with every confrontation of script, you must avoid confronting your client's process script until she has *closed escape hatches* congruently (recall Point 7). This caution is especially important in the area of counterscript confrontation, because the presenting issues the client is bringing in this area are usually apparently far removed from questions of suicide, homicide or going crazy. Nevertheless, if you do confront these counterscript issues, the client is likely to have to face up to the underlying issues in the script proper, and these may indeed involve one of the tragic script outcomes.

The importance of modelling by the counsellor

To be potent in inviting process script change, you have to model it by staying out of your own script process as far as possible during sessions. This demands also that you stay out of driver behaviour. Recall that *driver invites driver* (Point 18). Thus each time you show a driver behaviour, your client is likely to take this as an invitation to get into a driver in return. If she does so, she will reinforce her process script. The same thing is likely to happen if she gets into a driver and you respond by showing driver behaviour yourself. In either case, the person's understanding in Child is: 'It *does* get me my needs met to get into driver around here, so I'll be even more ready to do it the next time.'

Confrontations for each of the process script types

Stan Woollams and Michael Brown (1979: 213) have listed ways of confronting each of the process script types. I acknowledge my debt to them for originating most of the recommendations that follow.

I also pass on to you their counsel: 'Potent therapy results from effective and appropriate intervention strategies *combined with* script-free process' (Woollams and Brown 1979: 213; emphasis in original).

Until script

- Invite the client to work *now* rather than waiting until 'later'.
- In particular, convey that it is OK for the client to change *before* he has worked out every detail of his script, rackets and games.
- Keep the work short, and come out as soon as any significant move is achieved. Avoid the temptation to 'hang in there until you've got just one more change'.
- When working out a contract, be ready for the client's Child strategy of 'going around the houses' to avoid saying straight out what he wants. Be prepared to offer a specific contract rather than waiting for the client to come up with one.

Never script

- Stroke – immediately and lavishly – any active step that the client takes into autonomy, no matter how small.
- If the client withdraws, be prepared to initiate action yourself: move to the client, instead of waiting for her to come to you.
- Do not buy into contracts for 'deciding between alternatives'. Instead, work out with the client what he needs to *do* in order to reach the decision he has not yet been able to reach.
- Invite the client to say openly what he wants, what he is going to do to get it, and what he is feeling and thinking while he does so.

Always script

- Stroke the client's spontaneity and invite her (playfully) to use it as a means to desired change.

- Watch out for the client's pattern of repeating previous negative behaviours (in relationships etc.). Ask the client to use Adult: 'What evidence do you have that this time is going to be different?' and 'What can you do to make it different?'

After script

- End the work on a positive note; anticipate possible negative escalations later, and take steps to ensure the client has protection.
- A variant on this is to invite the client, within the counselling session, to move to the negative escalations *first*, and go on to get the positive things later.
- Stroke the client immediately after positive statements (before the *but* and the negative statement follows).

Almost script

- Confront the client's pattern of 'almost finishing', 'almost understanding', etc. Ask for contracts whereby the client *completes* what she sets out to do. Stroke the client when a task or contract is cleanly completed.
- During counselling sessions, finish the work before moving on to anything new. If a piece of work cannot be finished (because of time or the client's unwillingness to proceed) ask the client for a summary of what *has* been achieved.
- (For the Almost Type II pattern): confront the client's wish to hurry on to the next piece of work (inside or outside the counselling situation) without noticing that the previous piece has been completed. Stroke the client for what he has achieved, and invite him to celebrate each achievement as soon as he has made it.

Open-ended script

- Confront the Open-Ended pattern by inviting the client to use goal-setting techniques and to review her goals frequently, both for the longer and the shorter term.
- Reframe the script pattern by pointing out to the client that these 'blank pages' in her script are a gift in disguise: they are hers to fill in in whatever way she wishes.

Key point

Confront the *process* of your client's script, as well as its content. Confront script process not only by your interventions, but also in your modelling.

You can diagnose script process either directly, or by observing driver behaviour, or through your knowledge of the client's personality adaptation.

---

21 Make and keep contact: the Ware Sequence

Paul Ware (1983) distinguishes three possible areas of contact between counsellor and client. These *contact areas* are *thinking*, *feeling* and *behaviour*.

He suggests that to make effective contact with any given client, you need to address these three areas in a particular sequence. This *Ware Sequence* varies according to personality adaptation.

In this Point, I explain how you can use Ware's system to make and keep good rapport with your client.

Three 'doors to contact'

Each person, says Ware, has three contact 'doors': open door, target door and trap door.

Each person's contact doors correspond to the three contact areas of thinking, feeling and behaviour. However, the *order* of correspondence between contact doors and contact areas differs from one personality adaptation to another.

For example, for a person whose main adaptation is Sceptic, the Ware Sequence looks like this:

- open door: thinking;
- target door: feeling;
- trap door: behaviour.

By contrast, the Daydreamer's open door is behaviour, his target door thinking, and his trap door feeling.

In making first contact with someone, says Paul Ware, you need to address the area that corresponds to their *open door*. Once you have established communication at the open door, you can move to their *target door*. This is often the area in which most of the overt 'work' gets done in the course of counselling.

The *trap door* is the area in which the person is most heavily defended and is most likely to get stuck. However, Vann Joines (1986) suggests that it is also the area in which the client is likely to make her most profound personal changes.

If you address the doors out of order, the person is likely to block you. This is especially probable if you attempt to make first contact at their trap door. How do you know if they are 'blocking' you? The answer is that you look for driver behaviour. If you have addressed the wrong contact area for that client at that moment, the chances are that she will show a driver. She may then follow this by experiencing a racket feeling, and/or engaging in some form of scripty behaviour or thinking.

The Ware Sequence and personality adaptation

Table 21.1 shows the different orders of the contact areas in the Ware Sequence for the six personality adaptations.

Example: using the Ware Sequence with the Over-Reactor adaptation

With someone whose main adaptation is Over-Reactor, for example, you would make contact most effectively by first addressing her open door of feeling. As she comes into a session, you might open with a warm 'Hello! So, how are you feeling today?' You would not begin by asking her: 'Have you been thinking about what we did at our last session?' If you wanted to know that from her, you would wait until she had had a chance to expand to you about how she was feeling, then put your question.

An even more ineffective opening would be: 'What do you want to do in this session?' The Over-Reactor is likely to respond to that by beginning to feel bad. A person with this adaptation decided in childhood that her role in life was to please others by doing what they wanted. She decided also that she needed to

Table 21.1   *The Ware Sequence for different personality adaptations*

Adaptation	Open door	Target door	Trap door
Workaholic	Thinking	Feeling	Behaviour
Sceptic	Thinking	Feeling	Behaviour
Daydreamer	Behaviour	Thinking	Feeling
Critic	Behaviour	Feeling	Thinking
Over-Reactor	Feeling	Thinking	Behaviour
Manipulator	Behaviour	Feeling	Thinking

Source: Ware (1983).

read other people's minds to find out what she needed to do to please them.

Thus when you ask her what *she* wants to do, she may replay this childhood pattern. If so, she will begin wondering what you expect her to do. Then she may feel inadequate or confused because she fears she may not be doing the right thing to please you. If you persist in addressing her trap door of behaviour, she in turn will most likely escalate her racket feelings.

With this client, you will only make good contact in the area of behaviour if you have first gone through her open and target doors of feeling and thinking. You need to do this at the client's pace, taking care that she is moving with you. You can check this by watching out always for driver behaviour. If the client gets into a driver, or shows other script signals, your best option is to back-track and make good contact again at the previous contact door.

In fact, Vann Joines (1986) suggests that with many clients, you may *never* address the trap door directly. Often, he says, all the overt work of counselling gets done at the target door. However, the client is still likely to make his most significant script changes in the area of the trap door.

Testing for contact area

If you are in doubt about your diagnosis of personality adaptation, you can simply apply the Ware Sequence in trial-and-error style by making test interventions. If your client responds to you in a way that is free of driver behaviour or racket feelings, the chances are good that you have addressed the correct contact area for that client. By contrast, if the client gets into a driver or shows a racket, you have most probably chosen the wrong contact area.

For example, suppose that at the beginning of a counselling session, you decided to test whether the client's open door was behaviour. You might open by saying: 'If there's anything you want to do to get comfortable, please go ahead and do it.' If the client simply goes ahead and does things to get comfortable – takes off his shoes, rearranges the cushions, or whatever – you have probably made the right judgement.

However, suppose that instead of this, he arranges himself carefully on his chair, body vertical round the mid-line. He pauses and looks up at the right-hand corner of the ceiling, while pressing the fingers of both hands together in front of him. He replies: 'Well, I think, actually, I'm comfortable enough already, thanks very much.'

Noting these Be Perfect driver signals, you might judge that his main adaptation was Workaholic or Sceptic, not Daydreamer. This would mean that his open door is thinking, not behaviour. You therefore shift tack and retest with: 'OK, good. So, will you tell me what your thinking is in coming to counselling?'

Using the Ware Sequence in the long and short term

The Ware Sequence gives you guidance to both the long-term strategy and the short-term tactics of treatment. Over the longer perspective of the treatment plan, your client's main adaptation indicates the contact areas in which you will be likely to work most effectively with him in the early, middle and late stages of treatment.

For the client whose main adaptation is Daydreamer, for example, you might centre your early sessions on the fulfilment of behavioural contracts. Once the counselling relationship is well established, you can move with the client into exploring and clarifying his thinking. Later still, the client is likely to do his most significant change work in the area of experiencing and expressing feelings. This can happen even though you and he may never address the area of feelings directly.

From moment to moment within each counselling session, you can keep contact with the client by staying aware of his open, target and trap doors and addressing them in the appropriate sequence. By continually looking out for driver behaviour, you can track whether or not the client has moved with you.

Using the Ware Sequence: a seven-point summary

Here is an aide-memoire to using the Ware Sequence:

1   First assess your client's main *personality adaptation*. You can do this either by listing personality features (Table 19.1), or on the evidence of her primary driver(s) (Table 19.2), or both.
2   From your judgement of her personality adaptation, read off the sequence in which you need to address her three *contact areas* of feelings, thinking and behaviour (Table 21.1). You can check this by testing different contact areas and observing her response (this Point, above).
3   Make initial contact with your client at the *open door*.
4   When that contact has been established, move with the client to the *target door*.
5   The *trap door* is where the client is likely to make the most significant changes. This may occur while you are working with her at the target door.
6   Do not address the contact areas out of order. While you are addressing them in order, check continually that your client has shifted area with you. Make this check by looking out for driver behaviour. If the client has not moved with you, go back to the previous area in the sequence.
7   These recommendations apply both in planning your longer-term treatment sequence (strategy) and in choosing your interventions from second to second (tactics).

Self-supervision: contact areas and the Ware Sequence

Select a taped excerpt, between five and ten minutes in length, from a recent counselling session. Use a tape of a client whose personality adaptation you have already assessed (Point 19). Listening to the tape several times through, review each interaction between you and the client. Note the following:

- Which contact area are you addressing each time? How does the client respond? On this basis, assess which contact areas correspond to the open, target and trap doors for this client.
- Review your assessment of the client's main personality adaptation, on the evidence of her personality traits and of her driver behaviours (Tables 19.1 and 19.2).

- Review the sequence of contact areas predicted by Ware for this personality adaptation. Does this sequence fit with your own judgement of the client's open, target and trap doors?

Key point

Use the Ware Sequence of contact areas to make and keep effective rapport with each client.

---

22   Get on your client's wavelength: the five Channels of communication

In this Point I describe how you can enhance your communication with your client still further, by making an informed choice of *how* you say things.

Taibi Kahler (1979a, 1979b) asserts that to achieve clear communication, you can do more than simply *avoiding* driver behaviours. In place of drivers, Kahler says, you can actively choose to use any one of five *communication Channels*.

Kahler's word 'Channel' is a playful reference to amateur radio. You and I, says Kahler, may want to communicate with each other over the radio waves. But if you are on one wavelength and I am on another – if we are on different Channels – we are not going to communicate. To get on the same wavelength with you, I need to choose the Channel that matches yours.

In their literal meaning, Kahler's five Channels refer to the *process* of communication. That is, they are about how you say what you say.

As I shall explain later in the Point, you make your choice of Channel according to the other person's personality adaptation and primary driver.

The five Channels of communication

Kahler (1979b: 6–12) designates the Channels by numbers (Channels 1 to 5) as well as by descriptive names. Table 22.1 shows the characteristics of the five communication Channels. The Channels are ranged on the table with Channel 5 highest. This is to convey the suggestion that *intensity of stroking* generally increases as communication moves from a lower- to a higher-numbered Channel.

'Ego-state behaviours' and Channels

You will see in Table 22.1 that Taibi Kahler has labelled communication in each Channel in terms of TA's traditional 'functional ego-states' – Adapted Child, Nurturing Parent, and so on. In reality, this is shorthand for a more complex state of affairs.

The point of using Channels is to allow you to *choose* how you are going to say what you say. Since you are making this here-and-now choice, it follows by definition that you must in fact be in Adult, no matter what Channel you choose. However, you make a deliberate choice to use the typical *behavioural signals* of a particular 'functional ego-state', which (for all Channels other than Channel 3) is different from Adult.

For example, to initiate a communication in the 'Nurturative' Channel 4, you would adopt a quiet, warm tone of voice, smile at the client and lean forward towards her while saying whatever you wanted to say. All these would be typical behaviours of someone in the traditional 'Nurturing Parent' ego-state. In reality, you would be choosing your behaviours from Adult throughout.

Your client, of course, is likely to respond to this by actually moving into the ego-state shown in the table. Indeed, this is the objective of the communication. In this example, if your choice of Channel 4 is the right one, the client will move into a Child ego-state. Experiencing herself once again as a child, she experiences you for your part as the 'positive Nurturing Parent' whose behaviours you are deliberately choosing.

The descriptions of the Channels, and the example I have given, all assume that there is no discounting. In particular, it assumes that both parties stay out of driver behaviour. Thus in the example above, the counsellor's smile needs to be a real smile, not the teeth-bared grimace that is an indicator of the Please You driver.

Table 22.1   *The five Channels of communication*

Number	Title	'Ego-state' behaviours	Communication style	Example
Channel 5	Emotive	+FC – +FC	Open exchange of feelings	'I'm *angry* at you!' – 'Yeah, and I'm angry at you, too!'
Channel 4	Nurturative	+NP – +FC	Nurturing	'Would you like a big hug?' – 'Ooh, yes!'
Channel 3	Requestive	A – A	Asking, requesting	'Will you tell me what you want?' – 'Yes, I will.'
Channel 2	Directive	+CP – A	Directing, telling	'Make five copies, please.' – 'OK.'
Channel 1	Interruptive	+CP – +AC	Command (aimed at action or the senses)	'Stand still!' – (does so)

Source: Compiled by present author from Kahler (1979b).

Additional detail on behaviours for each Channel

Channel 5

Communicating on the 'emotive' Channel 5 means choosing to express your feelings 'straight from the shoulder' – the kind of behaviour that is traditionally associated in TA with the 'Free Child' functional ego-state. Indeed, an effective way into Channel 5 is simply to express to your client what you are feeling. If you are feeling angry with her, or sad about something she is saying, a Channel 5 communication would be for you to express this feeling openly. Notice that Channel 5 means *expressing* feeling, not just *reporting on* it.

It may well be that your feelings are part of your own Child experience. However, to stay in Channel 5, you need to monitor your expression in Adult, even as you choose the behaviours of a Child ego-state.

As part of this Adult monitoring, you need to check that your feeling is not a racket feeling. If you are feeling embarrassed, or guilty, or blameful, or any of the other thousand-and-one feeling labels that describe racket feelings, *do not* use this as a way into Channel 5. Were you to do so, you would be inviting the client into his own racket feelings, not using a Channel. Check, then, that the feeling you are going to express is one of the four authentic feelings – 'mad, sad, scared or glad' in traditional TA parlance.

Another activity that marks Channel 5 is *playing*. You can use your Little Professor to create ways of being gently teasing or jokey with your client – always, without discounting. This is particularly effective in communicating with people who have Critic as their main adaptation (see Table 22.2 below).

Channel 4

I have already given an example of a set of Channel 4 'nurturative' behaviours above. For this Channel, allow yourself to use the modelling you have seen from parents or parent-substitutes who were effective in nurturing. Again, always monitor from Adult to ensure you stay out of driver. The main risk in Channel 4 is that you may slip out of nurturing and into Rescuing, through the Please You driver.

Channel 3

This 'requestive' Channel means asking the other person something, or requesting him to act, think or feel in a certain way. Use the behavioural signals of Adult – especially an even voice tone, steady eye contact, and a body posture that is upright and balanced around the vertical mid-line. Be alert to ensure that you do not move into a Be Perfect or Be Strong driver.

It is useful to think of every Channel 3 sentence as finishing with a question-mark. Use your voice to convey this, by raising your voice pitch at the end of the sentence in an interrogative manner.

Channel 2

In this 'directive' Channel, you issue an instruction or directive. In other words, you *tell* the other person to act, think or feel in a particular way. You convey this by the behavioural signals of the traditional 'positive Controlling Parent' functional ego-state. For Channel 2, you need to use a decisive tone of voice, with the pitch moving downwards from start to finish of the sentence; in this Channel, you are telling, not asking.

You can use the word 'please' as part of a Channel 2 command, if you wish to soften its impact on the social level. It is your voice inflection and other behavioural signals, not words like 'please', that differentiate Channel 2 from Channel 3. To experiment with this, you may care to speak the sentence 'Sit down, please' in two different ways: once with the rising pitch that conveys a question, giving Channel 3; and once with the decisive falling pitch that expresses a (polite) command, hence is Channel 2.

Channel 1

The 'interruptive' Channel, Channel 1, is like Channel 2 in that it conveys a command. However, Channel 1 is a purposely abrupt *command* that is aimed purely at the receiver's *actions or senses*. Your intention is that she should obey your command in 'Adapted Child' style, without conscious thought or hesitation. The tone and pitch of your voice should convey an exclamation mark at the end of the command. Examples are:

- 'Sit down!'
- 'Look at me!'

Table 22.2 *Communication Channels for different personality adaptations*

Adaptation	Channel(s)
Responsible Workaholic	3 (or 2)
Brilliant Sceptic	3 (or 2)
Creative Daydreamer	2
Playful Critic	5
Enthusiastic Over-Reactor	4 (or 5)
Charming Manipulator	2 (or 4)
(Channel 1 is not specific to any adaptation.)	

Source: Compiled by the present author from Kahler (1979b); names of adaptations as in Joines (1986).

- 'Breathe!'
- 'Stop that!'

Channel 1 is for use in one rare circumstance only: to interrupt a potentially dangerous escalation in feelings or behaviour. For example, you might use it if your client began hyperventilating, or if she was about to rush out of the counselling room uttering threats of violence. Do *not* use the word 'please' when communicating in Channel 1: your aim is impact, not politeness.

Matching communication Channel to personality adaptation

When you know someone's main personality adaptation, you have an excellent guide to that person's preferred communication Channel. The correspondences are shown in Table 22.2 (Kahler 1979b: 33).

Example: using communication Channels with the Sceptic adaptation

Suppose you judge that your client's main personality adaptation is Sceptic. This indicates to you that you can best make initial contact with him through Channel 3, that is, by *asking* him something. For example: 'Will you tell me what you're thinking?' He will usually also respond positively to a simple *directive*, given through Channel 2, such as: 'Say what you're thinking.'

By contrast, what would happen if you were to try to make

contact with him through Channel 5? Suppose you opened playfully with a grin and: 'Hey! I bet that Little Professor of yours has a lot to say today!' Chances are that this person would 'crease up inside' and respond by getting into his Be Perfect or Be Strong drivers.

Testing for communication Channel

If you are not sure about your client's main personality adaptation, you can check her preferred communication Channel directly. You do this simply by addressing communications to her through various different Channels and noting how she responds. If the Channel you are using 'hits the mark', she is likely to respond to you also in Channel (usually the same Channel that you have used). If, on the other hand, you have used the wrong Channel for her, she is likely to show that by coming back to you with a driver behaviour.

As you will realise, this process of 'testing for Channel' is yet another way in which you can get a double-check on your diagnosis of the client's main personality adaptation – another 'way into' the Process Model.

Key point

Choose your Channels of communication to ensure that you stay 'on the right wavelength' with each client.

---

23 Bring it all together: the complete Process Model

In this Point, I bring together all the features of the Process Model and present them on a single diagram. Using a case illustration, I explain how you can use the complete Process Model as a rapid and reliable guide to treatment planning.

The complete Process Model diagram

Figure 23.1 shows the diagram of the complete Process Model (Kahler 1979a, 1979b). At first sight, this may seem a complicated picture. However, it becomes easy to understand when you realise how it is built up. It simply consists of all the various features of the Process Model that you have met in previous Points, spread out in 'layers' over a two-dimensional matrix. For example, each of the five drivers has its own place on the diagram. The same is true of each process script type, each communication Channel, and so on.

Thus the diagram gives you a 'map' that allows you visually to cross-relate different Process Model features one with the other. For example, suppose you locate the Workaholic adaptation (top right on the diagram). You can immediately read off four Process Model features of that adaptation:

- primary driver: Be Perfect;
- main process script type: Until;
- preferred Channel: 3;
- initial contact area: thinking.

You do not need to start by finding a personality adaptation on the diagram. You can start from any Process Model feature. For example, if you locate the Try Hard driver, you can confirm that it goes along with the Always process script and the initial contact area of behaviour. If you start by locating Channel 4, you can see that it will suit the person with a Please You primary driver, and so on.

The Assessing Matrix

The two-by-two matrix that forms the base for the Process Model diagram is called the *Assessing Matrix* (Kahler 1979b: 18–31). Its two axes relate to yet another aspect of personality, not mentioned in earlier Points. They portray the person's preferred style of approaching others in social situations.

The vertical axis shows an 'active-passive' dimension; the horizontal axis shows 'involving-withdrawing'. The words in these labels have specialised senses in the Process Model, as follows:

- *Active*: liking to initiate social contact.
- *Passive*: not liking to initiate social contact.
- *Involving*: liking to be part of a large group of people.

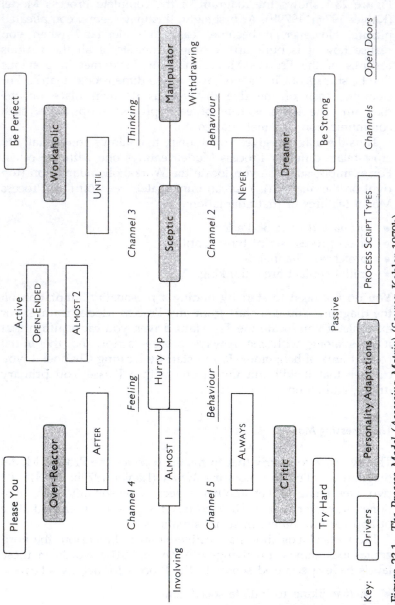

Figure 23.1 *The Process Model (Assessing Matrix) (Source: Kahler 1979b)*

- *Withdrawing*: liking to be either alone or with a few other people.

Thus the Assessing Matrix has four *quadrants* with the following meanings, working from the top-right quadrant clockwise:

- *Active-withdrawing*: moves proactively to initiate social contact. Prefers to relate to one person, or a few other people, at a time. Is happy in solitude.
- *Passive-withdrawing*: does not readily move to initiate social contact. Will respond to social contact if others take the initiative, but is also comfortable with solitude.
- *Passive-involving*: likes to be part of a large group, but does not proactively initiate contact. Typically, will move to the fringe of an existing group, then do something provocative or unexpected that cuts across their flow of communication. The psychological-level aim is to be pulled reactively into the group while maintaining a passive stance.
- *Active-involving*: proactively moves into large groups, or gathers a large group around her. The classic 'life and soul of the party'. Uncomfortable with solitude.

In my experience, these personality traits do not have the same wide diagnostic application as the other features of the Process Model. The most important function of these two axes, I believe, is to provide a base for the 'geography' of the Process Model diagram. However, the four quadrants do provide you with yet another means of cross-checking your Process Model reading for any particular client. You need the opportunity of observing the client as he moves towards others in a social situation. You may get some clues from his own reports of his relationships. Also, you can observe how the client initiates contact with *you* as he relates to you in the counselling room.

Using the Process Model as a guide to treatment planning

From Figure 23.1 you will see how the complete Process Model assists you in treatment planning. It does so in two ways:

1 It gives you a method of rapid *diagnosis*, through the observation of your client's primary driver.
2 It provides a way of checking, immediately and visually, that your *contract* and your *treatment direction* are congruent with your diagnosis.

From Part I.j, you will remember the 'Treatment Triangle'. It models the continual three-way interplay between contract, diagnosis and treatment direction. In Point 8, I stressed the importance of keeping an accurate *match* between these three main strands of your treatment plan. The complete Process Model allows you to make this match rapidly and reliably. It helps you also to keep a continual check on the accuracy of the match as treatment goes on.

The 'head-up display'

On some high-tech aeroplanes, the pilot has what is called a 'head-up display' of the instrument readings. These planes go so fast that the pilot doesn't have time to look down at his instruments. He needs all his attention to be focused on where the plane is going. Therefore, the instrument readings are projected on to his visor. He can read them with his head up, while still keeping his gaze on the airscape in front of him.

Whenever I am doing counselling or therapy, I make an imaginary 'head-up display' of the complete Process Model and keep it in front of my vision. Thus, as I attend to my client from second to second, I am looking at her 'through' the 'head-up display'. Transaction by transaction, I track the client and myself around the Process Model.

I suggest that you also make yourself a 'head-up display' to use in this way. While you are still getting accustomed to the Process Model, you may find it helpful to make a physical poster of Figure 23.1 and hang it on the wall of your counselling room.

Making the initial Process Model diagnosis

You can make your initial diagnosis of your client's personality adaptation during the first few minutes of your first meeting with him. You do this by observing his driver behaviours. As always, the content of your conversation is irrelevant. You can make your driver readings before he has spoken a word about his personal history or his presenting problem.

Case illustration

Robert had telephoned me asking for counselling. As always, I had asked him to call on me for an initial half-hour talk-through, without obligation on either side. This session had just begun, and Robert was outlining the problems he hoped to deal with in counselling.

As I listened to the content of what he was saying, I also took note of the process of his communications from one split second to the next. He would often look upwards and to the right during pauses, while making the 'steepling' gesture with his fingertips. As he spoke to me, he used frequent parentheses: 'as I was saying', 'as it were,' 'in a manner of speaking'. As he said these phrases, his voice tone was clipped and evenly-modulated. Observing these combined clues as Robert showed them, I noted them as signalling the Be Perfect driver (Table 17.1).

Less often, Robert would show the behavioural signals of the Please You driver. He did this mostly when he came to the ends of sentences. Then, just for a split second, he would squeeze his eyebrows up into his forehead, while baring his upper teeth in the Please You 'non-smile'. His shoulders would come up round his ears, his face would go down and his eyes would open wide so he could still look at me. His voice, just on the last few syllables of what he was saying, would rise almost to a squeak.

Robert seldom showed other driver signals. He did sometimes shift for a second or so into the expressionless immobility of Be Strong. He hardly ever showed Try Hard. When he signalled Hurry Up, with a wagging foot or tapping finger, this was always while he was showing another driver.

From these clues, repeated often during a two-minute sample of conversation, I felt confident in my reading that Robert's primary driver was Be Perfect. Checking my imaginary 'head-up display' of the Process Model, I read off that his main personality adaptation was Workaholic.

From Robert's Please You driver signals, I noted also that his next most important adaptation was Over-Reactor. In the case illustration that follows, I shall keep things simple by referring only to his main adaptation of Workaholic. In Point 24, I shall say more about how you handle multiple positions on the Process Model.

Matching contract to diagnosis

As you plan your contract-making, you will be considering both *process* (how) and *content* (what).

The content of your contract will of course depend greatly on the client's presenting problem, and on what she says she wants from counselling. At the same time, you can consult Process Model evidence about the typical content features of script for different personality adaptations (Tables 19.1–19.4). This will help give you advance notice of the general issues that may underlie this client's problems and wants, and that may therefore become the focus of contract-making as treatment goes on.

Planning the process of contract-making

In planning the 'how' of contract-making, you gain valuable guidance from knowing the client's Ware Sequence. Looking at the whole perspective of the treatment process, you may plan to begin with contracts that address the person's *open door*. When you and your client judge that she has changed effectively in that first contact area, you may expect to move on to contract goals that centre on the next contact area, the *target door* for that person. As she continues to work and fulfils contracts at that area, she may well make her most fundamental script changes at the *trap door*. Your contracts may never address the trap area directly. If they do, it will only be when substantial change has been made in the target area.

Case illustration

At the end of our introductory talk-through, Robert and I had contracted to work together. I began reviewing my initial treatment plan.

Robert's main personality adaptation was Workaholic. Consulting my 'head-up display' of the Process Model, I read off his most-favoured Ware Sequence. His open door would be thinking, his target door feeling, and his trap door behaviour (Table 21.1).

Thus as I began the process of contract-making with Robert, I was thinking in terms of setting up initial contract work at his open door, in the contact area of thinking. Some possible early contracts for him might be:

- 'To take time, before our next session, to think how I have been setting myself up to feel my familiar feeling of harassment. To note down my findings and bring them back to discuss with you.'
- 'To complete a Racket System analysis here in the session, and choose one way in which I will move out of the Racket System in the coming week.'

I expected that later in treatment, when Robert was ready, I would invite him into contractual work that would move from his open door (thinking) to his target door (feeling). For example, he might take session contracts like these:

- 'To tell you [counsellor] at least four times during this session how I'm feeling, whether or not I think there's any point in it.'
- 'To put my mother on a chair in imagination and express to her how I feel about her for commanding me not to be who I really am.'

Behaviour as a marker for thinking and feeling

You will recall that an effective contract needs to be sensory-based (Point 11). This is easy enough to arrange when the contract is in the contact area of behaviour. But how can you make a sensory-based contract for change in Ware's other two contact areas, thinking and feeling?

The answer is to use behaviour as a contractual *marker* for thinking or feeling (Point 13). I used it in this way in the examples above, where Robert's 'open door' was thinking. These were contracts that centred on thinking or on feeling, but that also specified behaviours to *mark* the completion of the contract.

It is important to specify a behavioural marker in this way whenever the contract centres on feeling or thinking. Only by including the behavioural marker can you ensure that the contract is sensory-based.

Matching treatment direction to diagnosis

Your diagnosis of personality adaptation leads you directly to a set of *initial* ideas about treatment direction. You read off these choices directly from your 'head-up display' of the Process Model. In planning your choice of interventions, you will once again be considering *process* (the 'how') as well as content (the 'what'). The Process Model gives you guidance in both these choices.

Case illustration: process aspects

I started from my judgement that Robert's main personality adaptation was Workaholic. This led me to plan some likely features of my initial treatment direction with him in the area of the 'how', the *process*. These were as follows.

First, I would be ready to confront Robert's main *process script type*, namely, the Until script (Tables 20.1 and 20.2). I would do this by communicating to him at all levels: 'It's OK for you to change and get what you want, *without* first having "covered the waterfront" of self-knowledge.'

Second, when the occasion arose, I would also be ready to confront the content of Robert's Be Perfect *counterscript belief* directly (Table 17.2). In my modelling and in verbal content, I would convey to him: 'You are OK as you are, even if you sometimes make mistakes.'

Third, I would bear in mind Robert's preferred *Ware Sequence* of thinking, feeling, behaving (Table 21.1). I would apply this sequence immediately in my moment-by-moment communication with him, whatever the content of our communication might be.

At the same time, I would plan to apply that Ware Sequence also in our longer-term work. I have outlined this longer-term sequence in the section above on 'Contract-making'. I would plan to begin with work that entailed thinking and analysis. When Robert and I had made secure contact at this open door, I would expect to invite him to move to his target door with some feeling work. As that work progressed in its turn, I would expect to watch for his most significant changes at his trap door of behaviour. He and I might or might not ever address this third area directly.

Fourth, in the earlier stages of our work together, I would most often communicate with Robert through his favoured *Channel*: number 3, Requestive (Tables 22.1 and 22.2). In other words, to get through to Robert on his own wavelength and in his own way, I would ask him to think with me. Later on, if he shifted to feeling work, I might also test shifting Channel. I might then offer him nurturing around his feelings. That is, I would use Channel 4 in the contact area of feeling.

Case illustration: content aspects

I expected Robert's presenting problem to come from the content of his *counterscript*. And in fact, it turned out that he had come to me because he was becoming uncomfortable with his pattern of intractable overworking. Along with this went chronic fatigue, muscular tension and acid indigestion. Robert had already had these symptoms checked by his doctor and had been cleared of any underlying physical disorder.

Robert might have come wanting my advice on 'how to become a more comfortable frog'. He might have wanted me to help him get even more work done each day, or get it done without any mistakes. Had he done so, my Process Model knowledge would have helped me avoid going off with him down this anti-therapeutic side-track. However, Robert had already moved beyond this point before he came to me. He wanted help with 'stopping working so hard'.

Below this counterscript pattern, I expected, would lie earlier and more fundamental issues in the *script proper*. Thinking of Robert's Workaholic adaptation, I brought to mind his most likely injunctions (Table 19.3). In his childhood, he was likely to have heard prohibitions on being a child or enjoying himself, on being close to others, or on feeling emotions, especially joy or sexuality. I planned that, as Robert and I continued to work together, I would help him explore which of these injunctions had been most limiting for him during his later life.

He was most likely to be amenable first to thinking about this (working at his contact door). Therefore, I planned to ask him as a working assignment to buy and read a good introductory book about TA. I would ask him to look at the chapter on scripts and work out which injunctions he thought might be most typical of himself. I expected that later on, working at his target door of feeling, I might invite him into some redecision work, using two-chair technique or an early scene. He might then express the held feelings he had been harbouring about these parental prohibitions.

Dealing with Don't Exist

With Robert, as with all clients, I knew that his injunctions might well include Don't Exist. The Process Model does not contain specific clues for identifying Don't Exist. Nor does this injunction attach particularly to any one personality adaptation.

But in any case, I had no intention of waiting to see if the issues of suicide, homicide or go crazy would surface overtly in my work with Robert. Instead, when he was ready, I would ask him to close escape hatches (Point 7).

Continuously revise your treatment plan

All these predictions 'read off' from the Process Model make up an *initial* diagnosis and treatment plan only. This initial reading, of course, is tentative. You could think of it as a sketched road-map, with many of the details pencilled-in only roughly. You can be sure that as your work with the client goes on, this map will need a great deal of revision and refinement.

In part, you will do this refinement by using further methods of diagnosis. For example, you may carry out a full script analysis (Point 6). This will give you a more detailed reading of the client's script content than you could get from your Process Model predictions. A Racket System analysis would give you extra information about your client's script patterns in present time (Erskine and Zalcman 1979; Stewart 1989: 15–29).

Largely, however, the way to refine your treatment plan is to start using it, and then continually revise it. You begin by making tentative initial sketch plans of a treatment direction, based on your initial Process Model diagnosis. This is what I did in the extended case example in this Point.

You then start applying these tentative ideas. As you do so, you continually observe the feedback you are getting from your client. This gives you further evidence about the accuracy of your initial diagnosis, which you may then revise. As you do so, you revise your planned treatment direction accordingly; then you begin to apply the revised plans, observe further feedback – and so on.

This is the central message of the Treatment Triangle. Diagnosis, contract and treatment direction are never static. Nor are they independent of each other. Instead, they continually flow and interact, with a change in one being reflected in a change in one or both of the others. The complete Process Model gives you a reliable road-map to use in keeping track of these changes.

Key point

Use the Process Model to give you an initial *match* between your diagnosis of the client, your contract, and your treatment direction.

Expect to revise this three-way matching process continually as your work with your client proceeds.

---

24 As your client moves on the Process Model, move with her

This Point describes a more advanced application of the Process Model. If you are new to the Model, you may like to read this Point and then come back to it once you have built up some Process Model experience.

In describing the Process Model so far, I have spoken as though the client belonged at one and only one position on the Model. For example, I have presupposed that someone 'has' a primary driver of Please You. This implies that she also 'has' a main personality adaptation of Over-Reactor. In turn, this carries with it the predictions that she will 'have' a Ware Sequence of feeling, thinking, behaving, and will favour communicating through Channel 4, Nurturative.

These data in themselves are of great use in both diagnosis and treatment planning. However, for even more precise use of the Process Model, I am now inviting you to relax the assumption that people can be placed at one and only one position on it. Instead, you can be aware that in practice, the person may *move* from place to place on the Process Model. In this Point I suggest that when your client does move around the Model, you can improve your effectiveness by *moving with her*.

Short- and long-term movements around the Process Model

These movements on the Process Model are of two distinct kinds: *short-term* and *long-term*.

By 'short-term' movement, I mean that the person may shift from one part of the Model to another between one moment and the next. For example, at one moment she may be showing the drivers, contact doors and Channel preferences that fit the Sceptic adaptation. A second later, she may change to the signals of the Dreamer adaptation.

'Long-term' movement, by contrast, is seen only in people who are achieving script change. This may be through counselling or psychotherapy, or may happen in response to some other significant shift in life patterns. As the person changes, she will show shifts in her driver patterns. Along with these will go corresponding shifts in personality adaptation, preferred Channel, and Ware Sequence. In the second section of this Point, I shall describe the patterns of these long-term movements around the Model.

Following the client in short-term movements: case example

One of my supervisees reported that he was having difficulty in tracking his treatment direction with one of his clients. Every time the counsellor felt he was 'getting somewhere', he said, the client would somehow shift her ground and the progress of counselling would grind to a halt.

In supervision, we analysed this problem in terms of the Process Model. When making his initial Process Model diagnosis, my supervisee had noted that the client most often showed the behavioural signals of the Be Perfect driver. He had therefore concluded that the client's primary adaptation was Workaholic, with the Ware Sequence of thinking, feeling, behaving, and the preferred Channel being 3, Requestive.

However, as we listened to tapes of my supervisee's work with his client, we became aware that the client sometimes changed this pattern. In place of Be Perfect as primary driver, she would begin showing Try Hard. My supervisee realised that he had been discounting these changes, because, of course, he had already decided that the client 'had' Be Perfect as her primary driver.

We also made the interesting observation that these shifts in primary driver did not happen at random moments. Instead, the client would typically make such a shift just at the time when she was beginning to face up to a particularly important change in her script.

I suggested to my supervisee that he test out a new pattern of intervening when his client showed this shift of primary driver. Whenever the client showed Try Hard, the supervisee should act as though the client's primary adaptation were Critic, not Workaholic. Thus, he should adopt a Ware Sequence of behaving, feeling, thinking, and should use communication Channel 5, Emotive. My supervisee agreed to test out this strategy.

At the next supervision, he reported that when he had first used the new approach, it had 'worked like a charm'. When the client had shifted from Workaholic to Critic, my supervisee had shifted with her and kept contact. The client had gone on to make a significant redecision.

But in the next session, the supervisee said, he had seemed to lose touch with the client again. This time, with the understanding he had developed from our first supervision, he had made another check on the client's driver signals. Sure enough, the client had shifted back again from Critic to Workaholic. Once again, the supervisee had shifted Channel and contact area to suit, and he reported that the work again went ahead effectively.

Sometimes, as in this example, a client will shift between primary adaptations at crucial moments, as a way of defending her script. (This motivation for the shifts may only become apparent after the event, in supervision.) Occasionally, clients shift more rapidly, without obvious script motivation, so that they appear to be changing primary driver and adaptation literally from moment to moment in a session.

Luckily, there is a 'rule of thumb' that makes it relatively simple to keep track of this kind of shift. It is as follows: Transaction by transaction, choose your Channel and contact area to fit the driver that the client has just shown.

For example, whenever the client shows the Be Perfect driver, assume for that split second that she is in a Workaholic adaptation. Therefore, choose your immediate response so that you employ Channel 3 (Requestive) and follow the Ware Sequence of thinking, feeling, behaving. If, at the next transaction, your client shows the Be Strong driver, then *immediately* shift your response behaviours so that you are using Channel 2 (Directive) and following the Ware Sequence of behaving, feeling, thinking.

This may seem complicated at first sight, but a little practice soon makes it feel automatic. As an aide-memoire, here are the correspondences between the driver behaviours which the client may show, and the Channel and contact areas that you should use in immediate response:

Driver	Channel	Open door	Target door	Trap door
Be Perfect	3, Requestive	Thinking	Feeling	Behaving
Be Strong	2, Directive	Behaving	Thinking	Feeling
Try Hard	5, Emotive	Behaving	Feeling	Thinking
Please You	4, Nurturative	Feeling	Thinking	Behaving
Hurry Up	4, Nurturative	Feeling	Thinking	Behaving

Whether you address the open door or the target door will depend, as ever, on how far along you and the client are in your work together. If you address the target door and find that you get another driver behaviour in response, then, as usual, go back to the open door.

Movement on the Process Model in the longer term

As the person changes in the course of counselling, she is likely to show typical changes in her positioning on the Process Model. The essential nature of these changes is that the person *gains more options* among the repertoire of behaviours, thoughts and feelings that mark the various personality adaptations (Kahler 1979a: 28–30; Kahler 1995, personal communication).

Typically, the person will start off with one personality adaptation which, at the beginning of counselling, is clearly her main one – her 'home base'. As she progressively makes personal changes, she will become more and more at home in a second adaptation also. Note that she *does not lose* the characteristics of the original adaptation; she can still use them as fluently as before. As she changes still further, she may move into yet a third adaptation, while retaining her ability to 'be at home' in the first two.

When I speak of 'the repertoire of a personality adaptation', I mean not only its typical characteristics (recall Table 19.1) but *all* its Process Model features. Thus, the person who is in his 'home base' adaptation of Workaholic will show Be Perfect as his most frequent driver behaviour. His Ware Sequence will be thinking, feeling, behaving. His preferred Channel will be number 3, Requestive. His script beliefs and typical racket feelings, though not so readily predicted, will be likely to correspond quite closely to those that are typical of the Workaholic adaptation (Tables 19.3 and 19.4).

When the person extends his repertoire to his second adaptation, say Over-Reactor, he will not lose any of these features of the Workaholic. But, relatively more often than before, he will *also* show the Please You driver. He will be readily contactable on an additional Ware Sequence of feeling, thinking, behaving. He will gain the ability to feel comfortable with communication on Channel 4, Nurturative. In the content of his script, also, the typical issues of the Over-Reactor will join those of the Workaholic.

What if the person continues with personal change and moves into his third additional adaptation, say Dreamer? He will then in turn add Be Strong to his frequently-shown drivers. With that will go a Ware Sequence of behaving, thinking, feeling, and a facility for communication on Channel 2, Directive. The person's script content issues will widen out still further to incorporate those typical of the Dreamer adaptation.

How predictable are long-term movements?

When he was first developing the Process Model, Taibi Kahler believed that people would move from their 'home base' through two other adaptations in a predictable order. This order differed according to which 'home base' adaptation the person was starting from (Kahler 1979a: 31–42).

Now, on the evidence gathered from Process Model profiles on over 200,000 cases,[1] Kahler has concluded that the reality of long-term movement is more complex than this. His view now is that the person, starting from a 'home base' in any of the six adaptations, can move to *any* further adaptation(s) in *any* order (Kahler 1995, personal communication). Kahler now uses the term *phase change* to describe the way in which the person moves from one adaptation to the next, while still keeping the repertoire of the previous adaptation(s).

His present findings indicate that you cannot predict the order of such long-term phase changes by any predetermined rule. Instead, you need to stay aware of the possibility of these long-term movements through adaptations, and look out for them when you are making your diagnoses. Bear in mind especially that, by the very fact of being in counselling, your client is likely to be making script changes. As she does so, she is likely also to make phase changes on the Process Model.

Taibi Kahler recommends that in treatment, you should make initial contact with your client at her 'home base' adaptation. Then, if she makes a phase change, the focus of your work with her should move to the issues attaching to the *new* adaptation – that is, the one she has just moved into.

Implications for diagnosis

From this description you will see that, as a person achieves more and more personal change, you will find it more and more

---

1 For some years past, Kahler has been developing a computer-generated system of personality profiling, designed for clinical application, known as the Transactional Analysis Script Profile (TASP). It is based upon the Process Model, as well as upon Kahler's earlier work on the Miniscript (Kahler 1974). This validated profiling system identifies and cross-relates many items of script, including: ego-states, transactions, games, personality structure, phases in life, psychological needs, drivers, rackets, defence mechanisms, roles, positions, early decisions, six modes of perception, failure mechanisms, major impasses, and underlying script tissues. Additionally, it indicates effective therapeutic techniques and intervention strategies (Kahler 1995, personal communication).

difficult to 'place' her on the Process Model. This has immediate significance if someone comes to you for counselling who has already done substantial personal-change work. You may find that initial Process Model diagnosis seems difficult and 'diffuse' in such a case.

However, you can turn this apparent problem into an advantage. You can bear in mind that this client *has many more options* for both receiving and giving out communication than does another person who has stayed in just one well-defined, solid 'home base' on the Process Model.

Implications for treatment direction

With a client who has moved and developed many options within the Process Model, you can use several moment-to-moment approaches that I have described in this and previous Points. It is particularly useful for you to track shifts in driver behaviour and respond to each driver with the corresponding Channel and contact area, from second to second, in the way I have described in the previous section of this Point. You can also continually test for contact area and test for Channel (recall Points 21 and 22).

In planning your longer-term treatment direction, you can bear in mind the recommendation from Taibi Kahler that I have just given. Realise too that this client is likely to be less invested than most others in a particular Channel or Ware Sequence. That means that you may be able to move relatively soon to the person's target door, rather than needing to spend significant time making initial contact at the open door. This can apply even if the client has not worked personally with *you* during most of the change work he has done. The client may in fact invite you to his target door actively. If he does so, without showing driver behaviour, the thing to do is of course to follow him.

Key point

Once familiar with the basic Process Model, you can add the insight that some clients may move around the Model. This movement may occur from moment to moment, or it may take place in a longer term as the person achieves script change.

If your client does move around the Process Model, be adaptable and move *immediately* with her.

Treatment Tactics

I think of treatment direction as comprising both *strategy* and *tactics*. By 'strategy', I mean the way you plan your interventions over the whole perspective of the treatment plan. By 'tactics', I mean the way you choose interventions from session to session and from moment to moment.

This final section is about tactics. There are two main themes that run through its six Points. One theme is *confrontation*: what, when and how do you confront? The other, interrelated theme is how the techniques and ideas of NLP (neuro-linguistic programming) can fruitfully be combined with those of TA. Specifically in Points 27 and 28, I explore TA applications of two NLP ideas: *time-frames* (Cameron-Bandler et al. 1985) and the resulting careful use of *verb tenses* (Andreas and Andreas 1987: 25–36). Point 29 describes an NLP technique, 'shifting the voice', which works beautifully for the TA purpose of resolving impasses. As well, in all six Points, NLP notions mingle with those of TA, as they have done throughout this book.

One of TA's strengths over the years has been its ability to take techniques from other approaches and fit them comfortably under its own theoretical 'umbrella'. It has also had techniques and insights to offer these other approaches in return. I believe we are only now beginning to realise the mutual benefits that will come from combining TA and NLP, and I hope these Points will help speed the process.

25 Encourage discomfort and confusion

'I don't feel comfortable with that.'

How often have you heard this response when you asked your client to act, think or feel in a particular way?

We are doing humanistic psychology, and we are all supposed

to be kind to each other. Thus the conventional response from you is something like: 'OK, if you don't feel comfortable, let's work out another way to do it.'

How would it be, though, if your response was: 'I hear you don't feel comfortable with what I'm suggesting. Will you go ahead and do it anyway?'

Or even just: 'Good!'

In this Point, I suggest that there are times when it is fine for you to encourage discomfort. I look specially at one kind of discomfort – namely, confusion.

Discomfort and personal change

TA trainer Shea Schiff (workshop presentation) teaches: 'There are times when you have to move through discomfort in order to get to greater comfort.'

I would add that there are times when someone has to move to a position of *permanently* greater discomfort to achieve lasting script change. Autonomy and comfort are not the same thing.

However, I believe it is wrong to assume that therapeutic change *must always* be uncomfortable (recall Point 1 on 'Presuppositions'). For example, I question the assumption that the person must somehow 'return to childhood hurt' if she is to achieve lasting change. Your art, I believe, is to know when the client's desired change is likely to involve discomfort and when it is not. If you can facilitate change while your client stays completely comfortable, so much the better. If the client does need to go into discomfort, then you may as well confront her with that sooner rather than later.

When is discomfort therapeutic?

Luckily, TA theory offers several decision rules that you can keep in mind as you consider whether a client's discomfort is likely to be therapeutic. You can ask yourself the following three questions:

1 Is the client's uncomfortable feeling a racket feeling or an authentic feeling?
2 If the uncomfortable feeling *is* authentic, is it a feeling that functions to solve a problem in an appropriate time-frame?

3   If 'yes' to (2): As the client expresses this discomfort, does she also bring in her current resources to actively solve the problem?

Is the uncomfortable feeling a racket feeling or an authentic feeling?

In Part I.c, I outlined the difference in TA theory between a racket feeling and an authentic feeling. A racket feeling is a feeling learned in childhood and used in grown-up life as a manipulative means of furthering the script. Thus it is never therapeutic for you to stroke an expression of 'discomfort' that takes the form of a racket feeling.

But, given that you do not stroke expression of a racket feeling, how *do* you respond to it? Paradoxically, one effective move is often to encourage the client to *heighten* his rackety discomfort (McNeel 1976; Stewart 1989: 150–1). In using a 'heightener', you invite the client to escalate the racket to ever higher and higher levels of discomfort. The aim is that the client's discomfort will eventually feel so far 'over the top' that she will spontaneously move out of the racket and into some authentic expression. With this intervention you are inviting the client to go *further into* and *through* her discomfort, not to stay out of it.

Is the client's authentic feeling one that functions to solve a problem in the here-and-now?

The four authentic feelings (recall Part I.c) are 'mad (angry), sad, scared and glad'. However, these four feelings are not always authentic. People can and do show rackety anger, sadness, scare and happiness, alongside the authentic versions of the same feelings. How do you tell the rackety from the authentic?

One way is to observe the client's driver behaviours (recall Point 17). If the client shows *no* driver behaviour immediately before he expresses one of these four feelings, then the feeling expressed is authentic. If he *does* show driver behaviour, then the feeling may be a racket or may be authentic.

George Thomson (1983) has suggested another way of making the distinction. He points out that authentic fear, anger and sadness all have a *problem-solving* function in the here-and-now. This function is closely bound up with the three time-frames: future, present and past respectively.

Authentic *fear*, says Thomson, functions to deal with *future* threats. If I see a suspect-looking person loitering in a dark side street, I feel a fear of attack. I respond by making sure to stay within sight of others in the well-lit main street. Thus I safeguard myself against a possible threat that belongs to the future. (As in this example, it may be the very near future.)

Authentic anger, according to Thomson, has the function of dealing with *present* intrusion, attack or insult. If someone jostles me carelessly when boarding a bus, I may feel anger and respond by asking him sharply to be more careful.

The authentic feeling of *sadness*, Thomson suggests, deals with problems of the *past*. These take the form of irretrievable losses. If a close relative of mine dies, my sadness is my response to the knowledge that I can never get him back again. This emotion lets me know that I am dealing with the here-and-now problem. I do so by filling the space in my 'internal map' that used to be occupied by my dead relative.

If the person feels fear, anger or sadness outside of its appropriate time-frame, suggests Thomson, then it is a racket feeling. For example, a person may spend a lifetime being angry at someone who has been dead for many years, waiting for them to 'change in the past' and be the person she wanted them to be. Another person may continually feel sad about terrible events that have not happened yet.

Thomson's scheme gives you another guideline on whether to invite a client further into discomfort. You can ask: does *this* discomfort – fear, anger or sadness – have a problem-solving function for the client, in the respective time-frames of future, present or past?

As the client shows this discomfort, does he bring in present resources to actively solve the problem?

As Bob Goulding (workshop presentation) has pointed out, it is not necessarily therapeutic to simply 'ventilate feelings'. People do not have a 'barrel of bad feelings' that they somehow need to empty. The reality, says Goulding, is that the 'barrel' may be bottomless. If the person does nothing but ventilate his feelings, he can do so for months and years and nothing will change. If he does want to change, then at some point he must *do* something new. He must use his here-and-now resources actively to solve his problem.

I believe that Goulding's caution applies just as much to the expression of authentic feelings as to the expression of racket feelings. Even with authentic feelings, the expression of the feeling in itself is not enough to solve the problem; I also have to do something about it.

The three examples above, for fear, anger and sadness, will illustrate this. In each example I had to bring here-and-now resources into play to solve the problems in the future, present and past respectively. For my fear to be useful to me, I had to actively respond to it – by crossing the street – and not just feel it. Similarly, I had to express my anger coherently to the man who had jostled me on the bus in order to encourage him to stop jostling me. To benefit from the healing effect of sadness, I had to use my here-and-now resources in a different way: I had to *let go*, in the here-and-now, of the loved object I lost in the past.

I suggest this gives you another guideline to use when your client moves into uncomfortable feelings during counselling. To judge whether the discomfort is therapeutic, you can ask yourself: 'Is this client simply feeling or expressing his uncomfortable feelings time and again, and not changing? Or is he using the discomfort as a cue for *action*? Is he using his here-and-now resources to solve whatever problem he is feeling uncomfortable about?'

At any time, you can offer the client a contract to make active use of these here-and-now resources.

The importance of authentic confusion

Standard TA theory regards confusion as always being a racket. I believe that this assumption is too sweeping. I suggest instead that confusion can *sometimes* be a racket; but that there is also such a thing as *authentic confusion*. I suggest too that you should confront racket confusion, as you would any other racket, but that you should stroke authentic confusion. For example:

> *Client*: I'm confused about what you just said.
> *Counsellor*: Good!

Does this mean that TA's traditional 'four authentic feelings' need to be increased by one? No, because confusion is not a feeling. Rather, you might call it a specific state of thinking. This fits with established TA theory concerning the nature of rackets. They entail scripty patterns of behaviour and thinking as well as feelings (Erskine and Zalcman 1979).

NLP guru Richard Bandler has praised the benefits of

confusion. For him, 'Confusion . . . is always an indication that you're on your way to understanding' (Bandler 1985: 83). I agree with Bandler's portrayal of confusion as a kind of mental shake-up. I believe it is necessary for the rearrangement of the person's internal map (or, in TA terms, her frame of reference).

Once again the practical question for you is: how do you distinguish authentic confusion (beneficial) from racket confusion (scripty)? As before, one useful check is to watch out for driver behaviours. If your client showed *no* driver behaviour before becoming confused, then he is in authentic and not rackety confusion. If he *did* show driver behaviour, then the confusion may be rackety or may be authentic.

If the driver was Try Hard, it is most likely that the subsequent confusion is a racket. This is one of the most common of all driver-racket sequences.

Happily, even if you are mistaken in your reading of your client's confusion, you can often be effective with an intervention that invites the client to heighten it. One option is the simple 'Good!', as in the example above. This sounds on the social level as though you are stroking a racket. However, even if the client's confusion *is* a racket, the effect at the psychological level is that of a paradoxical intervention. In Child, the client will have been expecting a Parental squelch (the expected negative stroke), not the straightforward approval he now hears. Alternatively, you can heighten with something like this:

Client: I'm feeling confused at what you said.
Counsellor: So how about going ahead and getting even more confused? Take as long as you need and get just as completely confused as you want to.

Key point

Be open to the possibility that any discomfort, including confusion, may be a road into therapeutic change.

Use the clues I have outlined in this Point to help you decide when discomfort and confusion are authentic and when they are scripty.

26 Know what and when to confront

'Only a fool sets out to confront every discount.'

So says respected TA therapist and trainer Shea Schiff (workshop presentation). Schiff is in a good position to speak, having been one of the team who developed the theory of discounting in the first place.

But, given that you are not a fool and that you therefore do not confront *every* discount, which discounts *do* you confront?

In this Point, I suggest a set of rules-of-thumb that will help you make this decision from moment to moment in a session.

Starting point for the Point

I am assuming that you already have the skills to *identify* discounts and redefinitions. (For reminders, see Schiff et al. 1975: 14–18; Stewart and Joines 1987: 173–93; Stewart 1989: 109–33.)

I shall also enter a reminder of what is meant by 'confrontation' in TA counselling. In brief, to *confront* is to say or to do anything that invites the client to move out of script. 'Confrontation' does not necessarily imply a harsh or attacking intervention. On the contrary, you can make effective confrontations in an empathic and caring style (see the coming Point).

Seven questions on confrontation

I suggest that there are seven questions that you can ask yourself when deciding whether to confront. They are approximately hierarchical. That is, you should examine and clear the earlier questions in the list before going on to the later ones.

When you answer the first three questions, you will get clear rules about confronting. That is, '*Only* confront when . . .' or '*Do not* confront unless . . .'. Your answers to the other four questions will provide not rules, but flexible guidelines to confrontation. In these cases, knowing when to confront remains an art rather than an exact science. The questions are as follows:

1   Do I have a *contract for script change* with the client?
2   Has the client congruently *closed escape hatches*?
3   Is the discount to do with a *third-degree script payoff*?
4   Can I *collect useful information* about the client's script by not confronting immediately?
5   By not confronting immediately, can I open the way to *confront deeper issues*?
6   At what stage is the *relationship* between myself and the client?
7   What is the *context* of the discount, in terms of my current treatment direction?

Do you and your client have a contract for script change?

The rule here is simple: *no confrontation without contract*. I believe this is especially important to keep in mind during the earlier steps of your treatment plan (recall Point 3). At intake, for example, or during script analysis, it may be tempting for you to confront script issues there and then; they are often so obvious to you and apparently so obscure to the client. But this is always a mistake. It breaches TA's philosophical principle of 'I'm OK, you're OK'. In Bob Goulding's famous phrase, if you begin confronting script before you have a clear treatment contract, you change from *therapist* into *the rapist*.

Has your client congruently closed escape hatches?

Even when you and your client have a clear contract for treatment, you should not confront *any* part of her script until she has closed escape hatches (recall Point 7).

The sole exception to that rule is if you are in a position to offer the client temporary physical protection against tragic outcomes. For example, in a 'marathon' where the group is together at all times, you might move immediately to confront an existence issue. Even then, it would be crucial for you to ensure *beforehand* that the client has further protection in place if the issue remains open at the end of the marathon.

Is the discount around a third-degree script payoff?

By 'third-degree', I mean a script outcome entailing death or tissue damage to self or others, child abuse, criminal activity, or going crazy. In all normal circumstances, you should immediately confront a discount around such issues. An example would be where the client gives a gallows laugh while speaking of a fatal car crash.

Can you collect useful information about the client's script by not confronting immediately?

Often, the problem a client initially presents will turn around her counterscript. However, on doing a script analysis, you will frequently discover that this counterscript issue 'covers' a deeper issue from the script proper. A classic example is the client who comes to counselling to be cured of overworking, but who turns out to have been using the overwork as a Child defence against the injunction Don't Exist (Goulding and Goulding 1979: 44–8).

If you suspect that some such set-up is at work, you may choose not to confront the surface issue immediately. Instead, you can let the client go on talking while you gather information on the possible deeper issue that is really at stake.

Another frequent example of this arises when you are deciding whether to confront a client's driver behaviour. You will recall from Point 17 that, when you confront a driver, you are confronting one of the client's counterscript beliefs. However, you may choose not to confront the driver immediately. Instead, you can wait for the client to move through the driver into a racket feeling. In this way you can gather information on the client's typical driver–racket patterns, and on the script messages that go with his racket feelings.

By not confronting immediately, can you open the way to confront deeper issues?

This point follows directly from the one before. Consider again the client who uses overwork as a means of scripty defence against Don't Exist. By not immediately confronting the overwork issue, you leave the way open to later confrontation of the more fundamental existence issue.

This said, your choice here usually comes down to deciding in what order to do things. If you do choose to confront the overwork issue first, then you can take it that the existence issue will surface sooner or later. This underlines yet again the over-riding necessity for establishing protection, and especially for checking escape hatches, before you confront script in *any* order.

*At what stage is the development of the relationship between
you and your client?*

Eric Berne spoke of 'game dosage' (Berne 1972: 349–51). In his
usual sardonic style, Berne suggested that if you confront the
client's games too early in the progress of treatment, the client's
Child reaction may often be simply to break off the relationship.
But, said Berne, if you do not confront soon enough, the client
may decide to leave anyway. In that case she may see you in
Child as an 'easy touch' who did not offer her enough of a
challenge.

Thus in deciding whether or not to confront, you should take
account of the strength of the relationship you have forged with
this particular client. As a *general* rule of thumb, the earlier the
stage of the relationship, the less you should confront, and vice
versa. If you confront the client's script material too early, even
after you have a firm contract, she may simply respond by
leaving. She may leave literally, by terminating counselling, or
metaphorically by withdrawing from the process of change.

The client's personality adaptation is relevant here. Berne
himself pointed out that with the paranoid (Sceptic) client, it is
especially important to refrain from confrontation until you are
on secure ground in the relationship (Berne 1966: 90). In my
experience, this is also often true of people with the Dreamer and
Critic adaptations. By contrast, relatively early confrontation often
works well with Over-Reactors, Workaholics and Manipulators.

*What is the context of the discount, in terms of your current
treatment direction?*

The question here is: 'If I confront *this* particular discount, will
my confrontation take us further along in the treatment direction
that I am currently following? Or would a confrontation at this
point just take me and the client off in pursuit of a "red herring"?'

Your current *treatment contract* can be a guideline here. For
example, if the contract between you and your client was about
her redeciding around 'Don't Think', you might choose to ignore
a discount of her ability to feel. I stress 'might'; the decision
would depend a lot on your detailed knowledge of her script.

Again, sometimes a client may show a driver behaviour while
making a major change in a deeper part of the script. If so, you
may choose to let the driver pass unconfronted. For example,
Jake's session contract was to express sadness to his father, whom

he had placed on a chair in imagination. For some minutes, Jake expressed racket indignation at his father for not having been the parent he had wanted him to be. Then Jake's voice and face changed. With tears in his eyes he said: 'Thinking about that makes me feel really sad, Dad', and burst out crying.

I could have confronted his Be Strong driver wording. But I did not; the context was wrong. Having taken permission to express how sad he felt, Jake could take time later to consider – if he still needed to – whether anything could 'make him feel'.

Key point

Since no one in practice can confront every discount, your art is to decide what and when to confront. You can use the seven guidelines in this Point to help you in your judgement.

---

27   Confront softly

In the previous Point I suggested guidelines on what and when to confront. This Point focuses on *how* to confront.

I suggest that you can confront in ways that allow you to be empathic and stay 'alongside' your client, while losing none of the confrontation's impact. I call this 'soft confrontation'.

'Soft' v. 'hard' confrontation

The terms 'soft confrontation' and 'hard confrontation' are my own. They do not appear in standard TA terminology. Nor are they totally distinct styles of confrontation; the one merges into the other. In essence, these two terms indicate differences in the *intent* of the confrontation. In soft confrontation, as I have said, the intention is to stay aligned and empathic with the client while confronting. Hard confrontation, by contrast, aims to cut strongly across the client's current beliefs, thinking, feeling or behaviour.

What do these differences mean in terms of TA theory? The following are two distinctions that (usually) mark out soft from hard confrontation:

1   In hard confrontation, you intend your intervention as a negative stroke to the client. In soft confrontation, you intend it as a positive stroke.
2   In hard confrontation, you cross the transaction. In soft confrontation, you keep the transaction complementary.

What must soft confrontation achieve?

Like any confrontation, a soft confrontation must invite the client to test his script beliefs against here-and-now reality. Yet it sets out to do so in the form of a positive stroke rather than a negative one. How is this possible? Will not the client hear any positive stroke as 'confirming' his script beliefs rather than confronting them?

The answer is that in soft confrontation you are aiming to do the following three things:

1   Acknowledge that you have heard and understood the client's current frame of reference (his internal 'map of the world').
2   Positively stroke the client for the *good intention* of whatever dysfunctional pattern he has just shown.
3   Indicate that this dysfunctional pattern is not the client's best option for getting this good intention met in the here-and-now.

You do not need to do all of this at the social level. Psychological-level communication may perform some or all of these tasks.

Techniques for soft confrontation

The skill of soft confrontation lies mainly in the verbal constructions that you use. These verbal devices sound much like straightforward reflection. However, they actually consist of reflection *plus* a set of systematic verbal shifts. You take the client's discount, turn it around a bit, then give it back to him in a subtly altered form.

These verbal shifts can entail one or more of the following four devices:

1   Reframing from 'everybody's problem' to 'your [i.e. the client's] problem'.
2   Shifting the client's account of the problem from 'accepted fact' to 'client's belief'.

3 Shifting the script pattern from present continuous tense to past tense.
4 Reframing from 'negative results' to 'positive intention'.

Reframing from 'everybody's problem' to 'your [the client's] problem'

Often, people in script will speak of dysfunctional behaviours or beliefs without specifying *whose* behaviours or beliefs they are talking about. From the language the client is using, you can often infer the internal discount: 'Doesn't everybody . . .?' or 'There's nothing anybody can do about this.' The appropriate soft confrontation is simply to reflect the stated difficulty back to the client in a sentence with 'you' in it. For example:

Client: It's difficult to think in that kind of situation.
Counsellor: Yes, I can see you've had difficulty about that.

Client: Standing up to talk in public is so embarrassing.
Counsellor: I can certainly hear how embarrassed you've felt.

You do not need to emphasise the word 'you' by raising the pitch or volume of your voice. On the contrary, the sentences will sound more empathic if you give the word 'you' its usual low emphasis.

Shifting the problem from 'accepted fact' to 'client's belief'

This is closely related to the previous shift. Here, however, the focus is on confronting the client's implied discount 'This problem situation is just how things are', or 'This is an established fact of life.' In your soft confrontation, you hand the client's discount back to her, rephrased as something *she believes* – or, more potently still, something *she has been believing*. You do this simply by inserting the verb 'believe' at a suitable point in the reflected sentence. For example:

Client: It's no good – people just don't want anything to do with me.
Counsellor: So: you've been believing that people don't want anything to do with you. And, I think, you've felt bad because you believed that, am I right?

Client: I'm just naturally a poor speller.
Counsellor: You've been believing you naturally can't spell well?

As before, it is best not to emphasise the word 'believe'. Instead, reflect the sentence with the emphasis on the same words that the client emphasised, and slip in the 'believe' on a lower pitch and volume.

Shifting the script pattern from present continuous tense to past tense

I have already illustrated this shift in all the previous examples. In response to 'It's difficult to think . . .', the counsellor replied: 'I can see *you've had* difficulty' (and *not* 'I can see you have difficulty'). You can confirm the same shift of tenses in the other examples.

On the psychological level, this shift in verb tense is a concrete acknowledgement of the fact that script patterns originated in the person's past. The whole point of counselling is to help them become aware that, in the present, they are *not* bound by the limitations of the script. I shall say more about the directed use of tenses in Point 28.

The shift of the script pattern from present to past can be underlined by adding a reference to the person's childhood. You can also use a phrase such as 'back then' that emphasises location in the past. For example:

> *Client*: It's the same old problem – I don't seem to be able to make friends with new people.
> *Counsellor*: Yes, I know that's a difficulty you've had. I'm willing to bet that when you were a kid, you took a decision not to make friends with people you didn't know. Maybe, back then, that decision was a very good way of looking after yourself.

Reframing from 'negative results' to 'positive intention'

TA presupposes that *all behaviours have a positive intention* for the person who is carrying out the behaviour (Stewart 1989: 15–17). This is implied in TA's philosophical stance of 'I'm OK, you're OK', as well as in the concept that scripts are 'decisional'. The problem with script is not its intention, but the fact that it leads the person to seek to satisfy that positive intention through outdated, dysfunctional strategies.

In soft confrontation, you can show that you hear the client's account of a here-and-now problem, while reflecting back the positive intention of the script behaviours. For example:

> *Client*: I have so much difficulty in telling my partner what I want from him.

Counsellor: Seems to me like you've found a great way of avoiding getting refusals from him. Is that right?

Client: I'll try to do what we agreed.

Counsellor: Well, 'trying' is a great way to make sure that you don't actually do it. Congratulations for not letting me push you about!

Reframing to 'positive past intention'

One particularly potent technique for soft confrontation is to combine the third and fourth of the approaches I have just described. Thus, in your apparent 'reflection' to the client, you systematically do two things:

1 You reframe from 'negative current results' to 'positive past intention'; and
2 You stroke the client for being so smart as to go for that positive intention 'back then'.

I have already given an example of this in the dialogue above that illustrated 'shifting from present continuous to past'. In that example, the past positive intention was implied rather than stated. Here is a more explicit use of the technique:

Client: I was sitting in the meeting all day yesterday, wanting to speak up, but I couldn't find anything to say.

Counsellor: I remember you told me that when you were a kid, your brothers and sisters would often squelch you for being silly when you said anything.

Client: That's right.

Counsellor: So maybe you decided it would be better if you said nothing at all?

Client: Yes, I think I did.

Counsellor: Well, I think you were really clever to decide that – it was a great way for you to avoid getting hurt, back then.

Key point

You can confront softly yet with full impact. Use the guidelines in this Point to create ways of soft confrontation.

28 Keep script insights in the past where they belong

This Point continues the theme of using verb tenses. This time, I focus not on confrontation but on an occasion for stroking. What do you say to your client when he verbalises an insight into his script?

As I shall explain, your natural urge to stroke his insight may sometimes lead you to risk stroking the script belief itself. By the directed use of verb tenses, you can avoid this risk and open a therapeutic 'exit' towards script change.

A guideline for using tenses

In choosing verb tenses, you can follow this three-part guideline:

- put *problems* in the *past*;
- put *resources and actions* in the *present*;
- put *outcomes* in the future.

This is yet another practical application of the three *time-frames* (recall Point 2). As shorthand for this directed use of verb tenses, I use the term *time-framing*.

Pulling script into the present: a discount

I hypothesise that when someone uses verb tenses 'out of time', this almost always indicates that they are *discounting* (recall Part I.g). One frequent instance of this 'time-slip' is when a client gets an insight into her script and tells you about it *in the present tense*.

Imagine this scenario: a counsellor and her client are doing some decontamination work. Perhaps they have been reviewing the client's script matrix or Racket System. As they talk together, the client has an 'aha experience' about one of his own script patterns:

> *Client*: You know, I've just realised something. I stop myself being important, because I'm scared it would kill my mother!

Pleased that this 'penny has dropped' for the client, the counsellor reflects back the insight:

> *Counsellor*: You stop yourself being important, because you're scared it would kill your mother!

On the social level, the counsellor is simply stroking the client's accurate insight into his script material. But at the psychological level, something quite different is going on.

As so often, the psychological-level message here is not 'covert'. On the contrary, it is right on the surface, in the literal meaning of the words that counsellor and client are using. Specifically, it lies in the verb tenses they employ.

Both client and counsellor have used the present tense. But the client is not stopping himself being important *now*. He is not believing this will kill his mother *now*. For sure, his insight relates to a script pattern that he *has shown* on many occasions. But these occasions are all in the past.

By using the present tense, the client is implying that he is engaged *at this moment* in a scripty pattern of belief and behaviour. But he is not, in fact, performing that pattern now. Thus his statement entails a *discount* of himself and the situation.

The counsellor, for her part, has reflected that same discount back to the client. She has thus left the discount unconfronted. Worse still: the client, in Child, is likely to construe her literal reflection as 'confirming' his discount. Thus the counsellor's response has been anti-therapeutic. Without meaning to, she has invited her client to reinforce his script.

How the present tense can indicate a script belief

It might seem at first sight as though the client's discount here is trivial. Does it really matter much if the client 'slips' from past to present when he is talking about one of his script patterns?

I believe it does matter. It matters because, in using the present tense, the client is not just making a single 'time-slip'. He is doing something more significant than that: he is implicitly stating one of his script beliefs.

Why is this so? The answer lies in a double meaning of the present tense. The client says, '*I stop myself* being important'. As always when someone speaks in the present tense, this means two slightly different things. First, it means 'I *am stopping myself* being important, right at this moment'. That is the meaning I have already drawn attention to.

However, the present tense also indicates 'now and in the future'. So, when the client says 'I stop myself being important', he is implying: 'I stop myself being important, now and in the future as well'.

This is equivalent to the statement: '*I'm a person who* stops himself being important'. And that is the client's script belief about himself.

By her literal reflection in the present tense, the counsellor has unwittingly 'confirmed' the client's Child perception of himself as 'someone who stops himself being important, and probably always will'.

In summary, therefore:

1   If the client verbalises an insight into his script in the *present tense*, his statement entails a discount. (The only exception would be if the client were literally acting out the script pattern at the moment he stated the insight.) He is also implicitly stating a script belief.
2   If the counsellor reflects the statement back to the client also using the *present tense*, then the client will most likely hear her in Child as 'confirming' both the discount and the script belief.

Using time-framing to confront the discount

You can avoid this pitfall by using time-framing. You simply need to alter the verb tense you use in your reflection back to the client. This is the shift you have already met as a 'soft confrontation' in Point 27. In place of the client's present tense, you use a past tense. The English language offers a particularly useful construction for this purpose, the one that goes 'You *have been doing* . . .'. Here is how the interaction looks when you put in this shift of tense:

> *Client*: You know, I've just realised something. I stop myself being important, because I'm scared it would kill my mother.
> *Counsellor*: You've been stopping yourself being important, because you've been scared it would kill your mother?

That would be the 'softest' form of the shift in tense. To underline it more strongly, you could respond like this:

> *Counsellor*: Well, that's what you *have* been doing. And that's what you *have* been believing.

Or you could really lean on the tense shift, like this:

> *Counsellor*: Well, you *have* been stopping yourself being important –
> until now! And you *did* believe you'd kill your mother – until now!

With any of these forms of words, you communicate that you
have picked up and confronted the client's self-discount, 'That's
the way I am and always will be.'

How time-framing gives you a therapeutic 'exit'

This use of time-framing not only allows you to confront the
client's discount, but also leaves you with a proactive 'exit' from
the interaction. In taking this 'exit', you do two things:

1   You consign the problem to the past.
2   You draw the client's attention to his present resources and
future desired outcomes.

Recall the original example I gave, where the counsellor did *not*
use time-framing. Instead, both parties used the present tense.
The client stated one of his script patterns ('I stop myself being
important, because I'm scared it would kill my mother'). The
counsellor reflected the client's words back to him in the same
tense. At the psychological level, both parties had then simply
agreed the scripty statement about the client's behaviour. From
that point, there was no obvious 'way out' of the interchange for
either counsellor or client. The matter was closed, and the parties
needed to think of something new to talk about.

Now contrast the exchange when you use time-framing to
place the problem in the past ('You've been stopping yourself
being important, because you've been scared it would kill your
mother.') By shifting the script pattern into the past, you put an
implied question to your client at psychological level: 'So what
now?'

If you want to, you can put this question in words. It flows
seamlessly from what you have already said:

> *Client*: You know, I've just realised something. I stop myself being
> important, because I'm scared it would kill my mother.
> *Counsellor*: You've been stopping yourself being important, because
> you've been scared it would kill your mother?
> *Client*: Yes.
> *Counsellor*: So, do you still believe you can kill your mother by being
> important?
> *Client*: [*laughs*] No, of course I don't.

Counsellor: OK, good. Do you want to go on stopping yourself being important?

In your first intervention, you time-frame the scripty pattern back into the past. By the questions you then ask, you first direct the client's attention to *present* reality, then invite him to begin exploring his possible *future* outcomes.

Sometimes it is not even necessary for you to verbalise these follow-up questions. Your client may make the script change spontaneously on the shift in tense, as in this case example from a weekend 'marathon' I ran. Sue had taken a contract to express anger in the group, but had not yet done so. She had an insight:

Sue: I've realised that what I do is to scrunch my anger down inside, instead of expressing it on the outside.
Ian: Well, at least, scrunching it down is what you *have* been doing – until now.
Sue: [*goes red in the face: jumps up and yells at me across the room*] Oh, shit, Ian, will you stop putting bloody words in my mouth!
[*Group members break into laughter and applause.*]

Key point

When your client verbalises an insight into her script using the *present* tense, reflect it back to her using the *past* tense.

By 'time-framing' in this way, you confront the client's implied discount, 'This is how I am and always will be.' You also leave yourself with an elegant therapeutic exit.

---

29   Deal with voices in the head

Eric Berne's final book, *What Do You Say After You Say Hello?*, includes a section called 'Voices in the Head' (Berne 1972: 368–71). There, Berne states his view that 'internal dialogue' is not a metaphor. It is real, in the sense that all of us literally hear voices in our heads.

In this Point I describe a technique called *shifting the voice*. It allows you to enter into the reality of internal dialogue with your client. You invite him to take charge of these voices that have been carrying on conversations in his head. As he does so, he is often able to make major and permanent movements out of his script.

This technique is particularly useful for resolving *impasses* (recall Part I.f). At these 'stuck places' in personal change, you will often find that the person's internal voices have got into an ongoing dispute in which neither side wins the day. One traditional way to tackle this kind of situation is by using 'two-chair work'. In this, the client puts the two internal figures on cushions in imagination and has them 'speak to' each other. The aim is that they resolve their dispute. The technique of 'shifting the voice' is an alternative to this well-tried redecision procedure. In my experience, 'shifting the voice' often works faster than two-chair technique. It produces script change that is just as lasting.

Internal dialogue is both real and unreal

Before going on to the details of the technique, I believe it is important to be clear about its conceptual basis. This turns on the paradox that internal dialogue is both real and unreal.

How is internal dialogue 'real'?

Eric Berne (1972: 368–71) has underlined the way in which internal dialogue is 'real'. We all continually, and literally, hear voices carrying on conversations in our heads. For much of the time, we keep these voices outside of our awareness. However, we can bring them into awareness at any time we want to, simply by listening to them internally.

If you are in doubt about this, you may like to test it with a simple experiment. To do so, read through the following instructions first, then put the book down and do the exercise.

Stop reading. Simply let yourself hear whatever *external* sounds you can hear. What sounds are you now aware of that you had not been aware of while you were still reading? Traffic noise or birdsong from outside the room? The sound of your own breathing?

Now, in the same way, direct your attention inside yourself. Listen to whatever *internal* sounds you can hear in your own head. Do not try to make anything happen; simply listen. What internal sounds do you now hear that you had not been aware of before? Do you hear voices? If so, what are they saying? Do you recognise the voices?

If you gave yourself a little time to listen internally, you will certainly have heard a voice or voices in your head. You did not 'imagine' the voices; you heard them, just as you heard the other sounds from outside yourself. It is in this sense that internal voices are 'real'.

How is internal dialogue 'unreal'?

In another sense, it is self-evident that internal voices are *not* 'real'. I do not literally have my mother, father, siblings, or childhood versions of myself sitting around in my head talking with each other.

Thus, internal dialogue is 'unreal' in that the internal figures who 'speak' the internal dialogue are the person's own constructions. They are not real-life people who inhabit external reality. For example, the 'mother' who talks to me inside my head is not my actual mother. She is a figure of my own making, and her 'voice' is a voice of my own making.

The paradox

We thus have the paradox that internal dialogue is, at one and the same time, real and not-real. I believe that it is important in practical counselling to understand both sides of this apparent contradiction. This means that you stay aware of both the reality of internal dialogue *and* its unreality.

Many of the therapeutic techniques used in TA (as in Gestalt) deliberately play along with the metaphor that the internal figure *is there in reality* (cf. Berne 1961: 259). This is true of traditional 'two-chair work'. It is equally true of 'shifting the voice' (see below) and of any other approach in which the client externalises internal dialogue. To be fully congruent in facilitating work of this kind, you need to get right 'into the metaphor' with your client. As far as you are concerned, while the client is having a conversation with the 'mother' in his head, then the person he is hearing in there *is* his mother. The voice he is hearing *is* his mother's voice.

Yet in another part of your mind, you must continually stay aware that the internal figure is *not* there in reality. The person generating 'mother's voice' is *not* the client's mother. It is the client himself, speaking as the figure of 'mother' that *he* has created and that *he* keeps around in his head.

The risk in practice is that you may forget the second part of this mental balancing act. It is easy to get so engrossed in the work that you let the metaphor supersede the reality. You then begin fully believing, along with your client, that the internal figure is objectively real.

In that event, you lose much of your potency. So long as you truly believe the client's mother is really there, and that it really is mother's voice you are both hearing – then, of course, all you or the client can do is listen to mother and perhaps negotiate with her. Frequently, she will just continue to sit there, saying the same old things she has said in the past. It can be a long and tough struggle to persuade her of anything new.

By contrast, what new possibilities do you and your client discover when you keep in mind that 'mother' is *not* real? That 'mother's voice' is a voice that the client himself creates?

One interesting discovery is that this voice is not, after all, a 'voice from the past'. It cannot be, because the person from the past is not really here. Indeed, she may have died many years ago. Thus, every time the client hears 'her voice' in his head, it is a voice *he himself* is generating. For sure, he may be making the voice say things that he once heard his mother say in the past. But he is not generating the voice in the past; he is generating it right now, in the present.

Furthermore, since mother is not really there in his head, it follows that it is the client himself who is *choosing* to generate 'her voice'. Therefore, he must have some motive for generating it. This leads to some interesting questions. For example: if 'mother's voice' is continually scolding the client or screaming insults at him, how come he chooses to keep on creating an internal voice that says such nasty things?

Summary

When you are using any technique that addresses internal dialogue, it is important to bear the following four points in mind:

1 The voices your client hears in her head are 'real', in that she really hears them.

2 However, she does not have 'real' parents, or child bits of herself, sitting around talking in her head.

3 The voices she hears are voices that *she* creates, from moment to moment in present time. *She* puts the voices there. It is *she* who can decide whether or not to keep them there.
4 Since she creates the voices, she can take control of them. If she doesn't like some of the things they say, she can have them say different things.

Shifting the voice

The technique of 'shifting the voice' is drawn from NLP (e.g. Bandler 1985: 69–80). The procedure can be divided into two parts, which flow seamlessly into one another. Each part can alternatively be used on its own.

In the first part, you invite your client to pay detailed attention to the *submodalities* of the internal voice – its location, timbre, volume, and so on. When he has specified these, you invite him to change them one by one. For each change, you ask him to report his emotional reaction to the new quality of the voice. The aim is for him to eventually remake the voice in such a way that he no longer feels a racket feeling in response to it. The first part of the exercise is complete when his emotional reaction to the voice changes to either calm indifference or non-rackety hilarity.

Case example

In a group session, Morris had made an overall contract that he would redecide his outdated childhood decision 'I'm not important'. To mark this change, he had taken an in-session contract to stand up and brag about himself to the other members of the group. But when the time came for him to do this, he had felt tongue-tied and embarrassed. The session went on as follows:

> *Ian*: Morris, I'm wondering: are you hearing anyone saying anything to you in your head just at the moment?
> *Morris*: [*listens*] Yeah. There's a voice saying, 'You'll never get it right. You'll just make a fool of yourself.'
> *Ian*: Uh-huh. What I'm thinking is, it might be useful for you to take some time to play around with that voice a bit – move it around to different places, hear it in different ways. Are you willing to take some time to do that? [*Asks for a session contract for the technique.*]
> *Morris*: Yes, OK. [*Accepts the contract.*]
> *Ian*: OK. So, will you listen to the voice again and tell us: where is it coming from?
> *Morris*: In my head.

Ian: Where in your head? Like, is it in the centre, or towards the back, or where?

Morris: [*listens*] It's halfway between my ears, just about here [*indicates a point nearer the back of his head*].

Ian: There, right [*copies his gesture*]. OK, so now, I'm wondering what the voice sounds like. Would you be willing to role-play it?

Morris: Yeah . . . [*gruff, staccato, loud, low pitch*] 'You'll just make a fool of yourself.'

Ian: Ah, so that's what it sounds like. So, now – will you test out making the voice quieter? Have it say the same things, but quieter. How do you feel about the voice now?

Morris: [*listens*] Um, doesn't make much difference.

Ian: OK, well, put it back as loud as it was before. How's about you put it in a different place now? Instead of there in your head. Where would you like to put it?

Morris: [*smiles*] I'll try my left elbow. [*Laughs*] Sounds a bit silly coming from there.

Ian: Right! OK, now will you test something else? When you were a kid, did you have a favourite cartoon character? Like Mickey Mouse, or somebody?

[*Morris nods*]

Ian: Who was it?

Morris: Woody Woodpecker.

Ian: OK, so now will you have the voice keep on saying the same things, and keep hearing it from your left elbow, but now just change the sound so's it sounds like Woody Woodpecker?

Morris: [*listens, then bursts out into loud laughter*] Oh, yeah! That sounds really silly! [*In a Woody Woodpecker squawk*]: 'You'll never get it right! You'll just make a fool of yourself!'

Ian: OK, good! Morris, are you willing to take an assignment on this? That whenever you start hearing that voice saying 'You'll never get it right', you just let it keep on saying that, but have it saying it from your left elbow in a voice like Woody Woodpecker?

Morris: [*still laughing*] Yes, sure.

Soon afterwards, Morris went on to fulfil his contract to brag in front of the group.

Caution: ensure protection before shifting voices

Though this technique can be quick, easy and often humorous, it nevertheless means that the client is moving out of part of his script. Therefore, as with any other script disruption, you must ensure *beforehand* that there is protection in place for the client (recall the 'three Ps' from Part I.k). In the case example, Morris was breaking the counterinjunction 'Get everything right' (Be Perfect), which he had received from his father. Had there not been adequate protection, this might have laid him open to some more damaging element of the script proper, in particular the Don't Exist he had received from his mother. However, I knew that Morris had closed his escape hatches securely before I asked him to do this piece of work. Thus the needed protection was already in place.

Discovering positive intention

Once the client has put the voice somewhere satisfactory, and made it sound the way he wants, you can continue the work by inviting him to ask the voice what its *positive intention* is for him. Again this stems from the presupposition, common to TA and NLP, that all behaviours have a positive intent for the person. Notice that you do not ask the client to analyse the voice's positive intention from Adult. You invite him to ask *the voice* itself, and wait to discover what 'it' answers.

Your task is to listen to the client's report of the positive intentions that the voice gives. At each statement of positive intention, you ask the client if he is satisfied with that intention on the part of the voice. You also make your own check, from your knowledge of the client's script, whether that stated intention sounds autonomous or scripty, and feed back to the client accordingly.

If the client is not satisfied, or the stated positive intent still sounds scripty, you invite the client to put another question to the voice: 'And what is the positive intention you have in wanting *that* for me?'

This sequence can be repeated as many times as necessary until the voice's stated positive intention is both autonomous and satisfying to the client. There will *always* be such an intention, even if it is the most basic of all: to keep the client alive.

Case example

Morris went on, at a later session, to enquire about his internal voice's positive intention. He reported that the voice first replied 'To keep you from turning into a showoff.'

Not satisfied with this intent, Morris asked the voice what its positive intent for him in *that* was. The voice told him, 'To keep you from being laughed at.'

At this point, Morris became aware that, as a grown man, he could at times be laughed at and could still feel OK about himself. (This was a significant piece of deconfusion in itself.) Telling the voice this, Morris again asked for its positive intention in wanting him not to be laughed at.

The voice replied, 'I want people to want you around, not reject you.' Morris then agreed with the voice that he could identify with that intent. At my invitation, he thanked the voice for its care in looking after him. He went on to negotiate with the voice some other and more growthful ways in which it could fulfil its good intention.

Key point

Realise that while 'voices in the head' are real for the person, they are also the person's own creation. She makes the internal voices that she hears. If she does not like what they say, she can have them say something different.

By inviting the person to shift and change the internal voice, you can facilitate them to make significant and permanent changes in their script.

---

30 If you split people, get them back together

In this final Point, I suggest that it is important for you to stay aware of the splitting that you invite in your clients.

When you do invite your client to 'split himself' into several 'parts', you need to do so contractually and with a clear therapeutic purpose. Above all, you need to make sure that you invite him to get himself back together before the end of the session.

Splitting is an integral part of TA

The deliberate 'splitting' of people is one of the most common devices in TA. The structural model of Parent–Adult–Child has a three-way split built into it, even in its first-order version (recall Part I.a). If you go to second- and third-order analysis, you can find ways of splitting the person into at least 15 different parts.

And the splitting is not only a matter of pure theory. In TA counselling, you routinely speak and act as though your clients were split into three or more parts. Eric Berne himself wrote: 'The trichotomy must be taken quite literally. It is just as if each patient were three different people. Until the therapist can perceive it this way, he is not ready to use this system effectively' (Berne 1961: 259).

Deliberate v. implicit splitting in TA technique

I believe there are two distinct ways in which TA practitioners invite their clients to split themselves. In one, the splitting is deliberate and explicit. This is exemplified by the technique of 'two-chair work' (e.g. Goulding and Goulding 1979: 44–9) or 'multi-chair work' (e.g. Stuntz 1973).

Alternatively, the practitioner may invite the splitting more subtly, by means of the language he uses. This second approach is the more ticklish to handle, because this language-based splitting may or may not be fully within the awareness of the practitioner himself.

My own preference is to use the first means of splitting, explicitly and under contract. I avoid the use of 'splitting language'. These are the choices I describe also in the present Point.

The therapeutic importance of 'rejoining split parts'

Why is it important for you to invite people to 'get themselves back together' after 'splitting themselves'? After all, the 'splitting' is only a metaphor. Your clients do not in reality walk out of your consulting room as three bits of a person.

One answer to this question lies in a common humanistic value-judgement. It is that 'being whole' is intrinsically better than 'being split'. I mean these phrases in the sense of self-belief, not of physical reality.

However, I believe there is a more pressing practical reason for the need to reintegrate. It is this: even though the 'splitting' process used in TA is metaphorical, the person in Child *takes the metaphor as reality*. Indeed, most of the therapeutic moves that you make in TA are intended to invite and utilise this Child belief. The metaphor of splitting is 'real' at the psychological level of communication. And, as Eric Berne stressed, it is this level that determines the behavioural outcome of transactions.

To summarise: if you successfully invite people to split them-selves, they will experience themselves as split and they will act split. This is exactly what you want them to do – in the controlled and safe setting of your counselling room. But it is a bad idea for them to step outside that setting and still act and feel split. To avoid this, you need to ensure that they get themselves back together before they go.

Reintegration after deliberate splitting

In two-chair or multi-chair work, the splitting is an explicit part of the technique. You have the person, for example, split off a Parent or a Child ego-state and 'put' that Parent or Child on another chair in fantasy. You have them physically move from one chair to the other and conduct a 'conversation'. While the other 'part' of the person is on the other chair, you enter into the metaphor with your client.

Therefore, techniques to invite reintegration follow the same pattern. Before the work finishes, you ask the client, still within the metaphor, to perform actions that will bring the split-off 'part' back together with 'the rest of themselves'.

The detail of these techniques is different as between split-off Parent ego-states and split-off Child ego-states. This is because of the different nature of these two categories of ego-state. Parent ego-states are echoes of *another person* from the client's past. By contrast, Child ego-states are aspects of *the client herself*, albeit at a past time. This leads to the following two guidelines:

1 For reintegration of Parent, you ask the person to take the projected figure off the chair or cushion.
2 For reintegration of Child, you ask him to take that other part of himself back into himself in some way.

In both cases, the most effective way of inviting the reintegration is to ask the client to perform an *active symbolic behaviour* (George Thomson, workshop presentation).

Reintegrating Parent ego-states

Suppose that the client has been talking to 'his father' on another chair. The dialogue seems to be at an end, and you have tested with 'Any more you want to say?' If the client confirms he is finished, you can give an instruction like this: 'OK, so now, when you're ready to, will you take Dad off the cushion? And, when you've done that, will you turn the cushion upside down to show you've taken him off?' If you are using chairs, you can ask the client to turn the chair around (or upside down) in the same way.

Sometimes the client will refuse to take the Parent off the cushion. Alternatively, the imagined Parent figure may move 'of its own accord' to a different part of the room. If at all possible, you should not allow the work to end there. A jokey approach, still working within the metaphor, is often effective: 'Hey, I don't want your mother left sitting around my workroom. If I let that happen with everybody, this place would soon be jammed full of mothers! So, come on, what are you going to do to get her out of here?'

Despite all your invitations, the session may end with the projected figure still 'hanging around' in your consulting room. If so, you *must* record this in your case notes and come back to it as soon as possible in the following session. Your aim is to ensure that the client, symbolically but actively, clears away the projected figure. Otherwise, at psychological level, the client in Child will proceed as though Mother or Father were literally sitting in the room during your subsequent counselling sessions.

Reintegrating Child ego-states

Suppose your client has come to the end of a dialogue with one of her Child ego-states. You then need to find a way of having the client move the projected part of self back into herself. If this process can involve seeing and hearing, as well as action, so much the better. For example: 'So, now you've finished talking with little Jean for now, will you look at her now on that other cushion? . . . Will you thank her for this time together, and hear her saying something back to you? . . . And now, in your own time, will you pick up little Jean on the other cushion, and would you bring her closer? . . . And now bring her right back into yourself?'

Either at the end of the work or at any time during it, the client may refuse to bring the Child 'part' back together with herself. Indeed, she may express hatred of the other 'part' and proclaim that she is going to 'get rid of it'. This is especially common in Type 3 impasse dialogues.

You should not allow the work to end there. In this situation, it is appropriate for you to be directive. You should simply tell the client the truth – namely, that what she is proposing is impossible: 'Judy, you *can't* "get rid of" that younger part of you. She's part of yourself, and she'll always be with you. So will you bring her back on to the cushion now?'

From that position, you may ask the client and her split-off Child 'part' to enter into a negotiation. Instead of simply 'getting rid of' the unwanted Child 'part', the client can ask her what she wants. The Child 'part', in turn, can tell the client what has been her good intention for the client's grown-up self.

Here again, if the session ends before the client has been willing to make the reintegration, you must record this in your case notes and come back to it in the next session.

Using language that invites splitting

Here are three examples of dialogue taken from tapes of TA counselling sessions. None took place during a piece of 'chair-work'. They simply formed part of the ongoing conversation between counsellor and client.

1 *Counsellor*: I think your Child is very angry just now – is she?
   Client: Yeah, she's furious.

2 *Counsellor*: What's your Parent saying to you about this?
   Client: Oh, he's saying 'You've got to get this right!'

3 *Counsellor*: You know, I think there are a lot of scared Kids in this room.
   Client: Yes. I'm about seven years old right now.

When the counsellor uses language like this, she is inviting the client to 'split himself' just as surely as if he were putting 'parts' of himself on two cushions. In the first two examples, the counsellor presupposes in her language that a 'part' of the client – a Child and a Parent ego-state respectively – has a separate existence. The client acknowledges the split by referring to the 'other part of herself' in the third person, as 'he' or 'she'.

In the language of the third example, the presupposition is that the client himself *is* a child. Since it 'is' a Child ego-state that 'is there' talking with the counsellor, it follows by implication that all the other 'parts' of the client must be somewhere else.

Avoiding 'splitting language'

This kind of 'splitting language' is not necessary in TA work. I prefer to avoid it, and I would counsel you to avoid it. When I want clients to split, I use explicit methods of splitting like two-chair technique, where the splitting is immediately visible, cleanly reversible, and done under contract.

'Splitting language' is an extremely powerful invitation to the client to split himself. Yet because it is not a formal and explicit method, it is easy for the counsellor to lose track of the splitting she has invited. She may even be unaware she has invited the client to split. Thus it becomes easy for her to invite the client to split himself without first getting a contract to do so. In a worst-case scenario, this could result in clients being 'taken apart' piece by piece and then left metaphorically scattered all over the counselling-room floor.

How can you avoid unwittingly using 'splitting language', when you want not to use it? Mainly by taking care to address your client as 'you', no matter which ego-state he happens to be manifesting at the time. You can avoid such phrases as 'your Kid', 'your Parent'. You can also refrain from using language that presupposes the client to be a child.

Key point

When you use therapeutic procedures in which you deliberately invite the client to 'split' herself, be sure to invite her to bring her split 'parts' back together before the session ends.

Be aware of any 'splitting language' that you may use in your exchanges with your client. Either use such language contractually and with clear therapeutic intention, or do not use it at all.

Afterword: Living the Therapeutic Relationship

Well, there they are: 30 practical suggestions on how to be effective with TA. I listed the Points in more or less the order you would address them in your treatment sequence.

As you read these 30 Points through, you were perhaps wondering: 'Is there some overarching principle, some general idea, that brings all these practical suggestions together in a satisfying way?' I believe there is, and I want to talk about it in this Afterword. It is the *therapeutic relationship*.

The main guideline for relating therapeutically, I shall suggest, is given by TA's philosophical assumption: 'People are OK'. I shall argue that you can make this philosophy operational – can live it out in practice – by following the principle of *seeking positive intention*. That principle, either directly or by implication, has underlain every technique and attitude I described in the 30 Points.

Presupposing the therapeutic relationship

You may find it a bit surprising that I should find my 'overarching principle' in the therapeutic relationship, since in the entire book up to now I have only mentioned it once. What is more, that mention was cautionary. In Part I.j, I said: 'The TA practitioner does *not* assume that the "counselling relationship", of itself, will necessarily bring about desired changes.'

In this Afterword, I stand by that earlier statement. However, I also believe that the therapeutic relationship is the matrix that 'holds' all effective interventions and all treatment planning. Without a therapeutic relationship, personal change can happen only by accident.

In taking this view, I am following the example of Eric Berne. He similarly cautioned against assuming that people could be 'cured by love' (Berne 1966: 63). In Berne's writings, the therapeutic relationship gets few explicit mentions. Yet it is clear to me, from my knowledge of all that Berne did and wrote, that he did not discount the therapeutic relationship. On the contrary, he *presupposed* it as a sine qua non of effective therapy. He simply took the therapeutic relationship for granted, and assumed his readers would do so too.

The scheme of this Afterword

This Afterword, unlike the 30 Points, is not intended as a cut-and-dried practical recommendation. Instead, it is a set of personal reflections. Some of them are clear in my mind, others are still in the process of forming. I put them forward as my ideas, knowing that your ideas may be different. I hope you will find these notions useful as jumping-off points for your own further thinking.

My own starting point is this: I believe that the therapeutic relationship is not 'something you have'. It is not even 'something you do'. Rather, it is *a way you live*.

In fact, there is something linguistically misleading even in the noun phrase 'therapeutic relationship'. What we are talking about is not a *thing*; it is a *process*. It therefore makes more sense to think of it not as a noun, but as a verb. To have a therapeutic relationship, you need to relate therapeutically.

And this leads on to the interesting question: how do you do that? How do you need to live if you want your relating to be therapeutic?

As I have said, I believe the answer is already contained in the first philosophical principle of TA: 'People are OK'. I think now that 'personal OKness' is not just a moral or mystical precept, but rather a style of living that can be described operationally. It is a 'how-to' that can be taught by one person to another and systematically practised. The essence of that 'how-to', I shall suggest, lies in the principle of seeking positive intention.

However, I want first to explore the role of the holding matrix, the therapeutic relationship, in which that principle will be applied. What *is* the connection between 'being in relationship' and 'being therapeutic'?

The conundrum of 'therapy in the relationship'

One thing is self-evident about counselling: *you cannot not relate*. By the very fact that you and someone else are sitting in a room together, you are relating. If you offer warmth and empathy to that person, and spend an hour just listening closely to her story, you are relating. If you consult a mental 'head-up display' of the Process Model and address the other person's contact doors with split-second precision, you are relating. Even if you and that other person were to turn away from each other and face the wall in silence for an hour, you would still be relating.

There is another proposition about relating that I think is equally self-evident. It is this: *not all relating is therapeutic relating.* This is simply another way of expressing what I said in Part I: that the 'counselling relationship', of itself, will not necessarily bring about desired changes.

Of course, this contradicts a belief which many counsellors hold with deep conviction: namely, that the counsellor–client relationship is the sole locus of cure. Lapworth (1995) succinctly states this belief when he says: 'The relationship *is* the psychotherapy'.[1]

While respecting the sincerity of this belief, I do not believe that it stands up to factual examination. If we do try to say that 'the relationship is the therapy', we run into a logical conundrum that, for me, puts the statement out of court. This logical puzzle runs as follows:

Let us start from the proposition that 'Therapy consists *solely* in the relationship,' or 'The relationship *is* the therapy'. This is equivalent to asserting: 'Therapy and relationship are the same thing.' In the symbols of logic, we can write this proposition with an 'identity' three-bar sign, as: 'Therapy $\equiv$ Relationship' (read as 'therapy is identical to relationship').

So far, so good. This is no more nor less than the pre-supposition we started with. However, in logic it is always possible to re-state an identity with the terms reversed. If $x \equiv y$, then necessarily also $y \equiv x$. Thus, once we have decided to say 'Therapy $\equiv$ Relationship', we must logically also say 'Relationship $\equiv$ Therapy'. Reading this latter expression out in more leisurely English, we get: 'Relationship is identical to therapy.' Or, in still other words: 'All relationships are therapeutic.'

This is where we begin to run into trouble. When anyone suggests that 'therapy lies solely in the relationship', they must also, by logical implication, be suggesting that 'all relationships

1 Phil Lapworth is a transactional analyst. However, I stand by the general statement I made in Part I: namely, that TA practitioners do not rely on the relationship alone to cure. Instead, they employ contractual method, systematic diagnosis, and directed treatment planning. Phil Lapworth's paper is in fact an excellent illustration of all three of these processes (Lapworth 1995).

are therapeutic'. To my mind, this latter statement is obvious nonsense. Apart from anything else, if it *were* factually true that all relationships were therapeutic, then nobody would need counselling or psychotherapy in the first place.

The 'two-way exclusion clause'

I believe that the connection between 'relating' and 'being therapeutic' is more complex, and less forgiving, than a simple one-to-one identity. Instead, it takes the form of a 'two-way exclusion clause'. That is to say, neither the relationship alone, nor the counsellor's technique alone, can consistently promote effective change. Each has the potential to negate the other; to avoid such negation, each needs the support of the other. To spell this out, first, no matter what the good qualities of the counselling relationship, it will not consistently promote desired change unless it is supported by appropriate technique and treatment planning on the part of the counsellor. And second, no matter how skilful the counsellor's technique and treatment planning, these will not promote desired change unless they are supported by the quality of the counselling relationship.

This brings to mind Eric Berne's 'third rule of communication': namely, that the behavioural outcome of transactions will *always* be determined by what is going on at the psychological level. Most often, technique and treatment planning will be expressed at the social level of the counselling relationship; the quality of that relationship will subsist mainly at the psychological level.

Seeking positive intention

We thus come back to the question: given that not all relating is therapeutic, what quality do you need to promote in a relationship to make it a therapeutic relationship? Or, to ask it in another way: how do you relate if you want to relate therapeutically? The answer, I suggest, lies in *seeking positive intention*.

I have already mentioned the principle of 'seeking positive intention' in several Points earlier in the book. There, it appeared as an element of specific techniques. You will recall from Point 29 how Morris asked the voice in his head: 'What is your positive intention for me in that?' Whenever the voice responded with an intention that Morris could not accept as positive, he asked the voice again, 'And what is your positive intention for me in *that*?'

Eventually, after several rounds of this question and answer, the voice named an intention that Morris could accept as positive and identify with. I pointed out that there will *always* be such an intention, even if it turns out to be a highly generalised goal like 'To keep you alive' or 'To get you the love of others'.

In Point 27, on 'soft confrontation', I described how you could stroke the person for the positive intent of their behaviour, even while confronting its dysfunctional nature in the here-and-now. I said in that Point too that a basic presupposition of TA was that *all* behaviours, thoughts and feelings do have a positive intention, no matter how problematic the means the person is currently using to achieve that intention. This was implied, I suggested, in TA's philosophical stance of 'I'm OK, you're OK', as well as in the assertion that scripts are 'decisional'. The person's early decisions were always made with the intent of surviving and getting needs met, and represented the best strategies the young child could work out to achieve that intention. In adulthood, the positive intention remains; the only problem is that the means-whereby are outdated.

What I am suggesting now is that you can apply this approach of 'seeking positive intention', not just as part of specific techniques, but as an overarching principle that you use proactively all the time you are relating to your clients. Indeed, I use this principle now as a starting point in my way of relating to everyone, not just to my clients. That is what I meant when I said earlier 'the therapeutic relationship is a way you live'. For sure, the way *you* relate to people outside your counselling room is none of my formal business in this book. However, I have found that it keeps things pleasantly simple to relate to everybody using the principle of 'seeking positive intention', so I pass the idea on to you to deal with as you please.

Making OKness operational

As I have said, I believe that 'seeking positive intention' is a way to operationalise TA's principle: 'People are OK'. That well-known phrase, as it stands, conveys only an abstract philosophical viewpoint. It is a 'statement of essence rather than behaviour' (Stewart and Joines 1987: 6). This is all very well, except when you come to ask yourself: 'So what do I *do* if I want to put this philosophy into practice?'

The TA literature, until now, has been short of answers to that question. Some TA people have felt, uneasily, that it might simply mean focusing on whatever seems positive about people and behaviours, and ignoring whatever seems negative. For 'ignoring', in TA terms, read 'discounting'.

Other writers, taking a more hopeful view, have suggested that 'I'm OK, you're OK' means separating the person from the problem. For example: 'At times, I may not like nor accept what you *do*. But always, I accept what you *are*. Your essence as a human being is OK with me, even though your behaviour may not be' (Stewart and Joines 1987: 6; emphasis in original). This formulation does make clear that we do not need to discount negative behaviours. However, it still does not answer the question: what do I do, in practical terms, to show acceptance of somebody's 'essence'?

To answer this question, I suggest, we simply need to replace the word 'essence' with 'positive intention'. We can then say: 'I may not like nor accept the way you are behaving. I may even not like nor accept some of the values you hold. But always, I accept that your behaviours and values will serve a *positive intention* that I can agree with, accept and honour.'

The benefits of seeking positive intention

What are the practical benefits of seeking positive intention? For a start, the principle generates many specific techniques. I have already mentioned that it is central to 'shifting the voice' (Point 29) and 'soft confrontation' (Point 27).

In using more traditional technique, too, seeking positive intention helps you to orient your interventions in effective ways. For example, take a common situation in chair-work, where the client on the home cushion declares a wish to 'get rid of' the nasty-seeming figure on the projection cushion. If you simply go ahead and facilitate the client to break off communication with 'Mother' or 'Father', or to get rid of a split-off part of herself, this often feels like a satisfying 'closure' to both client and counsellor. However, as Mellor (1980) has pointed out, this route always has a cost. It means that the client from then on will exclude part of her ego-state structure. But that internalised Parent figure, or that disowned part of the Child self, is something that the *client* has created. To exclude that part is to exclude resources that the client could potentially use for her own growth and benefit.

Better, then, to think in terms of seeking positive intention. Instead of 'getting rid of' or 'barring out' a part of the ego-state structure, you can encourage the client to discover its positive intention for her. She can then go on to negotiate ways in which this good intention can be fulfilled positively in the present. This in turn helps her to become reconciled with that part of self and reintegrate it.

As well as its role in underpinning interventions and techniques, seeking positive intention has value in the wider context of setting attitudes. When we take on board the idea that all parts of the ego-state structure have positive intentions, we can also realise that it is appropriate for us to be friendly with all those parts of self. No part of the person's ego-state structure is to be condemned or disowned.

No longer, for example, have we cause to insult Parental ego-states by calling them such names as 'Witch', 'Ogre' or 'Pig'. Instead, each internalised Parent figure stands revealed as just another parent, with good intentions at heart, even though they may have had some misguided or downright harmful ways of going about things. These good intentions can always be retrieved, so that the previously 'negative' Parent turns into a positive resource for the person.

As you consistently seek positive intention, you will find that words like 'blame', 'fault', 'sabotage' and 'resistance' automatically disappear from your vocabulary. The concepts they represent will, at the same time, disappear from your frame of reference. You will no longer ask yourself: 'Why is this client resisting change?' Instead you will ask: 'What is the client's good intention in not wanting to change in the way I'm inviting?'

This attitude of positive questioning, in turn, generates the positive orientation that I spoke of in Points 2 and 5. That is: 'Look forward to the outcome, not backward to the problem.' When you focus on positive intention, it becomes obvious there is no point in dwelling on the person's problems. Indeed, it turns out that the problems themselves are irrelevant to personal change, except as past data on what *not* to do. These 'problems' have simply been counterproductive ways that the client has been using to attempt to fulfil a positive intention. The client already knows very well how to perform these unproductive behaviours, so there is no point in discussing them further. Instead, the fascinating question to explore is: 'Now we know your positive intention, what can you do differently to achieve that intention more resourcefully, more growthfully, more autonomously than before?'

Seeking your own positive intention

So far, I have focused on the second half of TA's starting principle, namely 'you're OK'. But equally important, I believe, is the first half, 'I'm OK'. In practical terms, this means consistently seeking your *own* positive intentions, as well as your client's. This idea finds immediate application in the model of the Outcome Matrix, which I described in Point 10.

As well, in more general terms, seeking positive intention has the same constructive results for you as it had for your client. When you make a mistake or take a wrong turn in counselling, you will have no inclination to 'blame' yourself for that mistake. Indeed, you will realise it is impossible to blame yourself, because the word 'blame' has disappeared from your vocabulary. Instead, you can simply ask yourself: 'Given my therapeutic intention, how can I intervene differently to achieve that intention more consistently, more elegantly, more speedily?'

This, of course, is a parallel question to the one you are asking your client about *her* intentions and behaviours. It underlines the way in which you and the client are jointly engaged on a fascinating voyage of discovery. On this voyage, both of you will be guided by the beacons of *positive intention* and *desired outcome*.

As you convey to your client how all ego-state 'parts' of herself are at heart friendly to her, you can stay aware also that all the 'parts' of yourself are friendly to you. No part of yourself need ever be blamed, disowned or excluded from the process of counselling.

In that way, the practice of seeking positive intention leads naturally to personal congruence. It also implies unconditional positive regard, both for your client and for yourself. And that, I believe, is what we properly mean when in TA language we say 'I'm OK, you're OK'.

References

American Psychiatric Association (1994) *Diagnostic and Statistical Manual of Mental Disorders* (4th edn). Washington, DC: APA.

Andreas, C. and S. Andreas (1989) *Heart of the Mind*. Moab: Real People Press.

Andreas, S. and C. Andreas (1987) *Change Your Mind – and Keep the Change*. Moab: Real People Press.

Bandler, R. (1985) *Using Your Brain – for a Change*. Moab: Real People Press.

Bandler, R. and J. Grinder (1975) *The Structure of Magic Vol. I*. Palo Alto: Science and Behavior Books.

Berne, E. (1961) *Transactional Analysis in Psychotherapy*. New York: Grove Press.

Berne, E. (1964) *Games People Play*. New York: Grove Press.

Berne, E. (1966) *Principles of Group Treatment*. New York: Oxford University Press.

Berne, E. (1972) *What Do You Say After You Say Hello?* New York: Grove Press.

Boyd, H. and L. Cowles-Boyd (1980) 'Blocking Tragic Scripts', *Transactional Analysis Journal*, 10 (3): 227–9.

Cameron-Bandler, L., D. Gordon and M. Lebeau (1985) *The Emprint Method: a Guide to Reproducing Competence*. San Rafael: Futurepace.

Cowles-Boyd, L. (1980) 'Psychosomatic Disturbances and Tragic Script Payoffs', *Transactional Analysis Journal*, 10(3): 230–1.

Crossman, P. (1966) 'Permission and Protection', *Transactional Analysis Bulletin*, 5 (19): 152–4.

Drye, R., R. Goulding and M. Goulding (1973) 'No-Suicide Decisions: Patient Monitoring of Suicidal Risk', *American Journal of Psychiatry*, 130 (2): 118–21.

English, F. (1971) 'The Substitution Factor: Rackets and Real Feelings', *Transactional Analysis Journal*, 1 (4): 225–30.

English, F. (1972) 'Rackets and Real Feelings, Part II', *Transactional Analysis Journal*, 2 (1): 23–5.

Erskine, R. (1973) 'Six Stages of Treatment', *Transactional Analysis Journal*, 3 (3): 17–18.

Erskine, R. and J. Moursund (1988) *Integrative Psychotherapy in Action*. Newbury Park: Sage.

Erskine, R. and M. Zalcman (1979) 'The Racket System: A Model for Racket Analysis', *Transactional Analysis Journal*, 9 (1): 51–9.

Goulding, M. and R. Goulding (1979) *Changing Lives Through Redecision Therapy*. New York: Brunner/Mazel.

Goulding, R. and M. Goulding (1978) *The Power is in the Patient*. San Francisco: TA Press.

Guichard, M. (1987) 'Writing the Long Case Study', workshop presentation, EATA Conference, Chamonix (unpublished).

Holloway, W. (1973) 'Shut the Escape Hatch', *Monograph IV*, William D. Holloway MD.

Joines, V. (1986) 'Using Redecision Therapy with Different Personality Adaptations', *Transactional Analysis Journal*, 16 (3): 152–60.

Kahler, T. (1974) 'The Miniscript', *Transactional Analysis Journal*, 4 (1): 26–42.

Kahler, T. (1978) *Transactional Analysis Revisited*. Little Rock: Human Development Publications.

Kahler, T. (1979a) *Managing with the Process Communication Model*. Little Rock: Human Development Publications.

Kahler, T. (1979b) *Process Therapy in Brief*. Little Rock: Human Development Publications.

Lakein, A. (1973) *How to Get Control of Your Time and Your Life*. New York: Signet.

Lapworth, P. (1995) 'Transactional Analysis', in M. Jacobs (ed.) *Charlie: an Unwanted Child?* Buckingham: Open University Press.

McNeel, J. (1976) 'The Parent Interview', *Transactional Analysis Journal*, 6 (1): 61–8.

Mellor, K. (1980) 'Reframing and the Integrated Use of Redeciding and Reparenting', *Transactional Analysis Journal*, 10 (3): 204–12.

Mellor, K. and E. Sigmund (1975a) 'Discounting', *Transactional Analysis Journal*, 5 (3): 295–302.

Mellor, K. and E. Sigmund (1975b) 'Redefining', *Transactional Analysis Journal*, 5 (3): 303–11.

O'Hanlon, B. and J. Wilk (1987) *Shifting Contexts: the Generation of Effective Psychotherapy*. New York: Guilford.

Perls, F. (1971) *Gestalt Therapy Verbatim*. Des Plaines: Bantam.

Schiff, J., A.W. Schiff, K. Mellor, E. Schiff, S. Schiff, D. Richman, J. Fishman, L. Wolz, C. Fishman and D. Momb (1975) *The Cathexis Reader: Transactional Analysis Treatment of Psychosis*. New York: Harper and Row.

Southgate, J. and R. Randall (1978) *The Barefoot Psychoanalyst* (2nd edn). London: Association of Karen Horney Psychoanalytic Counsellors.

Steiner, C. (1966) 'Script and Counterscript', *Transactional Analysis Bulletin*, 5 (18): 133–5.

Steiner, C. (1974) *Scripts People Live: Transactional Analysis of Life Scripts*. New York: Grove Press.

Stewart, I. (1989) *Transactional Analysis Counselling in Action*. London: Sage.

Stewart, I. (1992) *Key Figures in Counselling and Psychotherapy: Eric Berne*. London: Sage.

Stewart, I. and V. Joines (1987) *TA Today: a New Introduction to Transactional Analysis*. Nottingham: Lifespace.

Stuntz, E. (1973) 'Multiple Chairs Technique', *Transactional Analysis Journal*, 3 (2): 29–34.

Thomson, G. (1983) 'Fear, Anger and Sadness', *Transactional Analysis Journal*, 13 (1): 20–4.

Ware, P. (1983) 'Personality Adaptations', *Transactional Analysis Journal*, 13 (1): 11–19.

Woollams, S. and M. Brown (1978) *Transactional Analysis*. Dexter: Huron Valley Institute.

Woollams, S. and M. Brown (1979) *TA: the Total Handbook of Transactional Analysis*. Englewood Cliffs: Prentice-Hall.

Index

Note: Page numbers in *italics* indicate tables and figures.

Compiled by Meg Davies (Society of Indexers)

action
    and goal 48, 67–8, 70, 78–9
    as in the present 27, 30–1, 33, 67
    and words 70
action contract viii, 66–70, 79, 169
    and markers for script change 89, 91
Adult ego-state 4–6, 8, 12, 15
    and communication Channels 143,
        145–6
    and contract context 100, 102
    and counsellor 40
    and cure 18
    and escape hatches 17, 42, 55, 56–7
    and goal-listing 46
    and markers of script change 90
    and the present 27
    and process scripts 136
    and script analysis 51
    and visualisation 103, 107
antisocial (Charming Manipulator)
        personality 123, 174
assignment, and contract 15, 89
autonomy 19, 135, 166
    and change of goals 95
    and positive intention 190, 203

Bandler, Richard 34, 78, 169–70
Be Perfect driver 10, 110, 116
    and Almost II script 131
    avoiding 119
    clues to 112, 113, 114
    of counsellor 57, 117, 146
    and counterscript 99, 117–18, 156, 189
    non-verbal signals 146, 153
    and Open-Ended script 131
    and personality adaptations 63, 126,
        127, 130, 148, 149, 160–1, 162
Be Strong driver 10, 110
    avoiding 119
    confronting 175
    of counsellor 146
    non-verbal signals 120, 146, 152
    and personality adaptations 63, 126,
        148, 161–2
behaviour

active symbolic 193–4
    and contact areas 137–40, 141, 149,
        154–5, 156, 159
    driver 10, 51, 96, 109–17, 131–3
    and ego-state 3–4
    responsibility for 13–14
belief, script
    and confrontation 18, 173, 176
    and fact 176, 177–8
    and personality adaptation 122, 127,
        129–30, 162
    and present tense 180–2
Berne, Eric
    and communication 14, 200
    and confrontation 174
    and contractual method 14, 65–6, 67–8,
        76
    and cure 18–19, 24–5
    and ego-state model 3–4
    and internal dialogue 184, 185
    and the present 30
    and scripts 7–8, 74, 130–1
    and social control 56
    and splitting 192
    and therapeutic relationship 197–8
birth myth 52
blame, and positive intention 203, 204
blocking, by client 138
boundaries
    and business contract 41–2
    clear and flexible 39–40, 93
    and ground rules 38, 40–1
Boyd, H. and Cowles-Boyd, L. 54–5

case notes
    availablity to client 14
    before and after sessions 62–3
    and escape hatch closure 58
    as 'front sheet' 59–64
    layout 59–62
    and lead-in description 62
    and self-supervision 64
Cathexis school 12
change, personal
    and autonomy 19

change, personal *(cont.)*
  and length of treatment 24
  and markers 66, 70, 87–92
  and presuppositions 26–7, 166
  responsibility for 13–14, 33, 104
  and time-frames 28, 32
  and treatment direction 15–16
  see also goals, listing; script, change
child
  and decisions 9, 11, 13–14, 17, 201
  and racket feelings 7, 52, 167
  and script 7–9, 13–14, 15, 122–3, 138–9,
    178
Child ego-state 4–6, 8–9, 11–12
  and communication Channels 143, 145,
    146
  and confrontation 173, 174
  and driver behaviour 134
  and escape hatch closure 56–7
  and Free Child 53
  and outcome goals 43, 46, 135
  and paradoxical intervention 170
  and the past 27, 181–2
  and resistance to script change 85, 86,
    95–6, 100, 102
  and script analysis 52–3
  splitting and reintegration 192, 193,
    194–5, 202
  and visualisation 107
clarity, in contract 66, 93–4
client
  in co-counselling 40
  and contractual method 14–15
  and Outcome Matrix 72, 73–6
  and responsibility for change 13–14, 33,
    104
  and responsibility for escape hatch
    closure 57
  splitting 191–6
co-counselling, and boundary-setting 40
Collinson, Laurence 78
communication
  and driver avoidance 117–21
  incongruous 6–7
  non-verbal 49–51, 53, 119–21
  open 14
  psychological-level 6–7, 73, 74–5, 176,
    181, 192, 194, 200
  social-level 6, 181, 200
communication Channels 142–8, *147*
  Channel 1 (Interruptive) 146–7
  Channel 2 (Directive) 146, 147, 161, 162
  Channel 3 (Requestive) 146, 147, 149,
    156, 160–2
  Channel 4 (Nurturative) 143, 145, 149,
    156, 159, 162

Channel 5 (Emotive) 145, 148, 160
  and driver behaviour 116, 121
  and ego-state behaviours 143
  and personality adaptation 122, 126,
    142, 147–8, 160–1
  testing for 148
  types 143, *144*
comparative, hanging 85, 92
confidentiality 16, 41, 59
confrontation 18, 62, 165, 171–5
  and client-counsellor relationship 174
  and contract 172
  and counterscript 116, 134, 173
  definition 171
  and escape hatch closure 134, 172, 173
  guidelines 173–5
  hard 175–6
  and personality adaptation 174
  rules 171–3
  of script content 130
  of script process 130, 134–7
  soft 175–9, 182
    and reframing 179
    techniques 176–9, 202
  and verb tense 182–3
confusion, as treatment tactic 166, 169–70
consent, mutual, in TA 15, 98
contact areas 137–42
  and driver behaviour 116, 138, 139,
    141
  and personality adaptation 122, 126,
    160–1
  testing for 139–40
contact door 38, 137–8, 199
  open door 51, 137–8, 140, 141, 154–5,
    156, 161
  target door 51, 137–8, 139, 141, 154–5,
    156–7, 161, 164
  trap door 51, 137–8, 139, 141, 154, 155
context of contract 66, 83, 97–102
  benefits of 98–9
  elicitation 100–1
  'invisible' 101–2
  specification 99–100, 107
contract viii, 13, 14–15, 65–108
  and assignment 15
  behavioural 78–9
  business 35, 36–8
    and boundaries 41–2
  and clarity 66, 93–4
  definition 14, 67–8
  and diagnosis 16, 153–5
  finishable viii, 66, 83–7
    achieving 86–7, 90, 92
    definition 83–5, 93–4
    importance 85–6

and flexibility 93–7
  benefits of 93–4
  and boundaries 66
  long-term treatment 94–6
  short-term treatment 96–7
'forever' 85–6
and front sheet record 61
and goals 47–8, 65, 66, 154
multi-handed 76–7
overall 15, 63, 88
  changing 95–6
  and marker for script change 90–1,
    92, 107
  and script analysis 50
sensory-based 66, 78–83, 84, 85, 90, 92,
    93, 155
  benefits 80, 103, 106–7
  check-points 80–3
and time-frames 31
treatment 35, 36, 37–8
  and confrontation 174–5
  direction 16
  and goals 47
see also action contract; context of
    contract; markers; outcome
    contract; session contract;
    visualisation and contract
control, social 18, 56
counselling, and psychotherapy ix
counsellor
  in co-counselling 40
  competency 15
  and contractual method 14–15
  and driver behaviour 117–18, 119–21,
    134
  and modelling of script process 134
  and Outcome Matrix 72–6, 204
  in personal psychotherapy 118
  and positive intention 204
  and script change 87–8
counterinjunctions 8, 10, 189
  and script matrix 53, 63
counterscript 51, 74, 99, 156–7
  confrontation 134, 173
  and drivers 116, *116*, 117–18, 127
Critic (passive-aggressive) personality
    123, 145
  and confrontation 174
  and Process Model 160–1
Crossman, P. 16
cure 18–19
  one-session 24–7
  script 18
  and therapeutic relationship 197–200
  transference 18

Daydreamer (schizoid) personality 123,
    159, 162
  and confrontation 174
  and contact areas 138, 140
decision
  and child 9, 11, 17, 201
  responsibility for 13–14, 178
decontamination 62, 180
description, lead-in 62
diagnosis
  and contract 16, 153–5
  and drivers 152–3
  initial 35, 36, 157–8
  and personality adaptations 123
  and Process Model 61, 151, 152–7, 160,
    163–4
  reviewing 30–1, 33, 37–8, 63, 158
  and standard diagnostic manuals 60,
    62, 63
  TA models 60, 61, 63
  and treatment direction 155–7
  see also Discount Matrix; DSM-IV;
    Process Model; Racket System;
    script matrix; symbiosis
dialogue, internal 10, 184–91
  of counsellor 57
  and overhearing 56, 115
  as real and unreal 185–8
  and voice shift 184–5, 186, 188–90
discomfort
  as authentic/racket feeling 167–9
  as treatment tactic 17, 165–70
Discount Matrix viii, 61
discounting 96, 143, 145, 202
  and confrontation 171, 172–3, 174–5,
    176–7, 182–3
  definition 12
  and verb tense 180–2
'domino theory' 34–8
doors see contact door
dreams, and script analysis 49
driver messages 10, 99
drivers
  avoidance 117–21, 134
  and behaviour 10, 51, 96, 109–10
    clues 111–12, 113–14
    and contact areas 116, 138, 139, 140,
      141
    and process script 131–3
    shift 164
  and communication Channel 142
  and confrontation 173
  and content 114–15
  and counterscript 116, 117–18, 127
  and diagnosis 152–3
  and feelings 167, 170

drivers *(cont.)*
  non-verbal signals 51, 119–21, 143,
    145–6, 152–3
  order 51
  and personality adaptations 51,
    109, 125–6, 127, 130, 140,
    159–61
  primary 112–13, 125–6, 127, 130, 131,
    151
    shifts in 160–1
  recognising 109–17
  and script 115
  and word patterns 118–19
  see also Be Perfect; Be Strong; Hurry Up;
    Please You; Try Hard
DSM-IV 60, 61, 63

early-scene work 33, 62
ego-state model 3–6
  and communication Channels 143,
    145–6
  and escape hatch closure 56–7
  and splitting and reintegration 191–2,
    193–6, 202–3
  and time-frames 27
  and transactions 6–7
  see also Adult ego-state; Child ego-state;
    Parent ego-state
emotions, authentic 7
empathy
  and soft confrontation 171, 175, 177
  in therapeutic relationship 199
escape hatch closure 16–17, 35, 54–8, 157,
    173, 190
  and Adult ego-state 17, 42, 55, 56–7
  early 55, 56
  and ego-state 17, 41, 56–7
  as ground rule 42, 55, 56
  guidelines 55–6
  hard/soft 58
  and incongruities 17, 36, 37, 57, 58, 134,
    172
  as routine 54–5
exit, therapeutic 183–4
experience
  and action words 70
  and behaviour 3
  and change 69

fact
  and belief 176, 177–8
  and presupposition 24–5
Federn, Paul 30
feedback
  client–counsellor 49, 158
  counsellor–client 17, 81

feelings
  authentic 7, 145, 166–9
  and contact areas 137–9, 141, 154–5,
    156, 159
  and contracts 69
  and ego-state 3–4
  racket
    and childhood 7, 52, 167
    and communication Channels
      145
    and confrontation 173
    and confusion 169–70
    and contact areas 138–9
    and discomfort 167–9
    and driver behaviours 10, 115
    heightening 167
    and internal dialogue 188
    and personality adaptations 122,
      126–7, 129, 162
  responsibility for 14
finishable contract *see* contract,
    finishable
flexibility in contract 93–7
  and boundaries 66
  definition 93–4
  long-term treatment 94–6
  short-term treatment 96–7
frame of reference 12
front sheet
  case notes as 59–64
  definition 59
  layout 59–62
  and markers for script change
    90–1
future
  and change 27, 28, 31–2, 43, 67
  and verb tense 104, 184
  see also outcome; time-frames

game analysis 3, 7, 50
Gestalt therapy
  and internal dialogue 186
  and redecision school 11
goals 43–8
  achieving 95
  and actions 48, 67–8, 70
  changing 95–6
  conflicting 45, 47
  and contracts 47–8, 65, 66, 154
  listing 35, 45–7, 95, 136
  and problems 43–4
  and wants 44–5, 65, 80
Goulding, Mary and Robert 9, 11, 33, 53,
    85–6
Goulding, Robert 96–7, 168, 172
Grinder, John 78

ground rules
  and boundaries 38, 40–1
  and escape hatch closure 42, 55, 56
  setting 35, 36, 37–8
group work 41, 62

'head-up display', and Process Model 152,
    153, 154, 155, 199
history-taking, and the past 30, 32
histrionic (Enthusiastic Over-reactor)
    personality 123, 138–9, 174
homework 15, 89
homicide, and escape hatches 16–17, 52,
    57
humanistic psychology 165–6
Hurry Up driver 10, 110
  non-verbal signals 153
  as secondary driver 113

impasse 62
  and redecision school 11
  and 'two-chair work' 186, 194
  and voice shift 165, 185
injunctions 8–9, 51, 99, 115
  Don't 9
  Don't Be a Child 9
  Don't Be Close 9, 87, 99, 127
  Don't Be Important 9
  Don't Be Well 9
  Don't Be You 8, 9
  Don't Belong 9
  Don't Exist 8, 9, 157, 173, 190
  Don't Feel 9
  Don't Grow Up/Dont' Leave Me 9
  Don't Make It 9, 63
  Don't Think 9, 175
  and personality adaptations 127, *128*,
    157
  and script matrix 53
insight into script 180–4
intake
  interview 35, 36–7, 39
  record 59
intention, positive 177, 178–9, 190–1,
    195
  benefits 202–3
  of counsellor 204
  past 179
  in therapeutic relationship 197, 200–2
intervention
  paradoxical 170
  see also treatment direction
interview, initial 35, 36–7, 39
intuition, counsellor 49, 50, 53

Joines, Vann 123, 138, 139

Kahler, Taibi viii n. 1
  and communication Channels 142–3
  and drivers 10, 115, 117–18
  and Process Model ix, 109–12, 163,
    164
  and process script 131

Lakein, Alan 45
Lapworth, P. 199
life positions 8, 50, 52
life-script *see* script
'Little Professor' 145, 148

madness, and escape hatches 16–17, 52, 57
Manipulator (antisocial) personality 123,
    174
markers for script change 66, 70, 87–92,
    155
  definition 89
  and evaluating desire for change 92
  formulating 90
  and 'front sheet' 90–1
  in-session/out-of-session 89
  and visualisation 107
Mellor, Ken 34, 202
Miniscript 163 n. 1
modelling 134, 156
'multi-chair work' 192, 193

neuro-linguistic programming (NLP) vii,
    78, 165
  and context 97
  and voice shift 188, 190

observation
  and driver behaviours 109–11, 113,
    131
  and escape hatch closure 57
obsessive-compulsive (Responsible
    Workaholic) personality 123, 127,
    140, 174
OKness, as TA principle 8, 13, 73, 156,
    172, 178, 197–8, 201–2, 204
open door *see* contact door
outcome
  and action 66–70, 78–9
  for client 72, 73–6
  for counsellor 72–6
  multiple 66
  renouncing 16
  and time-frames 27, 28, 31–2, 67,
    183–4
  visualisation 66, 80, 103–8
outcome contract viii, 34, 66–70, 79
  and marker for script change 89, 91
  and Outcome Matrix 66, 71

Outcome Matrix model viii, 66, 71–7, 204
    changing 76
    and multi-handed contract 76–7
    psychological level 74–6, 77, 117
    social level 71–4, 75, 76–7
Over-Reactor (histrionic) personality 123
    and confrontation 174
    and contact areas 138–9
    and Process Model 153, 159, 162
overgeneralisation 82–3
overhearing, in internal dialogue 56

paranoid (Brilliant Sceptic) personality 63, 123, 126, 137, 140, 174
Parent ego-state 4–6, 8, 11–12
    and communication Channels 143, 146
    and escape hatch closure 56, 57
    and goal-listing 46
    and the past 27
    and permission, protection, potency 16
    splitting and reintegration 193–4, 196, 202–3
parents, and script 8–9, 13–14, 51–2
passive-aggressive (Playful Critic) personality 123, 145, 174
past
    and early-scene work 33
    and history-taking 30, 32
    and personal change 27–8, 43
    and verb tense 104, 178, 182–3
Perls, Fritz 11
permission
    and counsellor 16
    in ego-state model 8, 51
personality adaptations 61, 109, 122–30
    changing 162–3
    and communication Channel 122, 126, 142, 147–8, 147
    and confrontation 174
    defining features 123, 124
    and drivers 51, 125–6, 127, 130, 140, 159–61
    and injunctions 127, 128, 157
    phase change 163
    and Process Model 149, 154, 162
    and process scripts 131–3, 133
    and racket feelings 122, 126–7, 129
    and script beliefs 122, 127, 129–30
    and script content 126–9
    six types 122–5
    and Ware Sequence 137, 138–40, 141, 156
personality style, and Process Model 149–51

Please You driver 10, 110, 112, 149
    and Almost II script 131
    avoiding 119
    non-verbal signals 114, 119, 143, 145, 153
    and Open-Ended script 131
    and Over-Reactor personality 138–9, 159, 162
potency, and Parent ego-state 16
present
    as time for action 27, 30–1, 33, 67
    and verb tense 104, 180–2
presupposition
    and fact 24–5, 166
    open/closed 25–7
problem
    and goals 43–4
    and outcome 33–4
    presenting 60, 156
    reframing 176, 177
Process Model viii, ix, 109–64, 199
    and Assessing Matrix 149–51
    and diagnosis 61, 151, 152–8, 160, 163–4
    diagram 149–51
    and drivers 10, 51, 109–17, 152, 164
    long-term movements 159, 162–4
    and script analysis 51
    short-term movements 159, 160–1
    and treatment planning 151–2
    see also personality adaptations
process script 10–11, 50–2
    After 131, 136
    Almost 131, 136
    Always 131, 135–6, 149
    characteristics 132
    confrontation 130, 134–7
    and driver behaviour 131–3
    Never 131, 135
    Open-Ended 131, 136
    and personality adaptations 131–3, 133
    time-scale 133–4
    types 130–1
    Until 131, 133, 135, 149, 156
program messages 8, 51, 53
protection 38, 96, 99, 136, 173
    of counsellor 40
    from Parent 16
    and voice shifting 189–90
    see also escape hatch closure
psychotherapy, and counselling ix

Racket System viii, 61, 180
    analysis 3, 7, 154, 158

rackets
  identification 50
  and personality adaptation 122,
    126–7
  see also feelings, racket
redecision 157
  as cure 18
  and escape hatch closure 57
  and markers 88–9
  and 'two-chair work' 186
  and voice shift 186
redecision school 11, 18
  and permission 16
redefinition, and script 11
referral, need for 16, 35, 36, 37
regard, unconditional positive 203
relationship, therapeutic 14, 15, 56, 174,
    197–204
  as conundrum 198–200
  and positive intention 197, 200–2
relaxation, and visualisation 103–4
relief, symptomatic 18
rules *see* ground rules

Sceptic (paranoid) personality 123, 126,
    159
  and communication Channel 147–8
  and confrontation 174
  and contact areas 137, 140
  and counterinjunctions 63
Schiff, Shea 166, 171
Schiffian school 12
schizoid (Creative Daydreamer)
    personality 123, 138, 140, 274
script 7–10
  content 10
    and confrontation 130
    and personality adaptations 126–9,
      158, 162
  and counterinjunctions 8, 10, 53, 63,
    189
  and counterscript 51, 74, 99, 156–7
  decisions 13–14, 178
  and drivers 115, 117
  and injunctions 8–9, 51, 53, 99, 127, 157,
    173, 190
  insights 180–4
  and life positions 8, 50, 52
  messages 8, 53, 126–7
  payoff 17, 52, 172
  and permissions 8, 51
  process *see* process script
  and program messages 8, 51, 53
  and redefinition 11
  and script cure 18
  theme 52

see also belief, script; discounting;
    process script; script analysis;
    script change; script matrix
script analysis 3, 8, 9, 17, 35, 48–54
  and diagnosis 158
  and outcome 75–6
  and personality adaptations 130
  preparation for 49–50
  questionnaire 48–9, 50–3, 126
  and time-frames 30, 32
script beliefs *see* belief, script
script change 15, 66
  and contract 172
  markers for 66, 70, 87–92
  and movement on Process Model 159,
    163
  resistance to 85, 86, 95–6, 100, 102, 203
  and verb tense 184
  and voice shift 185–91
script matrix viii, 8, 48, 49, 53, 61
Script System *see* Racket System
self-supervision
  and assessing personality adaptation
    125, 126, 129–30
  and contact areas 141–2
  and driver behaviour 120–1
  and 'front sheet' 64
  and presuppositions 26–7
session contract 15, 35, 37–8, 63, 155,
    188
  benefits 80, 103, 106–7
  check-points 80–3
  and flexibility 96–7
  and marker for script change 89, 90, 91
sessions, time-boundaries 39
splitting, client 191–6
  deliberate/implicit 192
  and language 192, 195–6
  and reintegration 192–5, 202–3
Steiner, Claude 14–15
Stewart, Ian 15
  TA Counselling in Action viii, 54, 89 n. 1
Stewart, Ian and Joines, V. 201–2
stroke 7, 9, 95
  and communication Channels 143
  negative 7, 170, 176
  and process scripts 134, 135–6
  and soft confrontation 176, 179, 201
  and verb tenses 180–4
structural analysis 3, 4
  second-order/third-order 4–6, 191
  see also ego-state model
structural model *see* ego-state model
suicide, and escape hatches 16–17, 52,
    57
switch of roles 7

symbiosis
    and diagnosis 61
    and script 12

TA proper 7
TA theory
    outline 3–12
    see also Cathexis school; redecision
        school
tape-recording
    and front sheet 59, 62
    in script analysis 49–50, 64
target door *see* contact door
therapeutic, definition ix
thinking
    and contact areas 137–8, 140, 142, 149,
        154–5, 157, 159
    and experience 3–4
Thomson, George 85, 167–8
thought, capacity for 13
three P's *see* permission; potency;
    protection
time-frames viii, 27–34
    and action and outcome 67
    and authentic feelings 167–8
    and goals listing 43
    practical applications 32–4
    and stroking 180
    and treatment planning 30–2, 165, 166
    see also future; past; present
time-framing *see* verb tenses
transaction 6–7
    complementary 6
    crossed 6
    ulterior 6
Transactional Analysis Script Profile
    (TASP) 163 n. 1
transference cure 18
trap door *see* contact door
treatment
    philosophy 13–14
    principles 13–19
treatment direction 15–16, 27, 151, 155–8,
    160, 164
    strategy and tactics 165
treatment plan viii, 24, 35
    and case notes 64
    and flexibility 94–7
    and individual session 37–8
    and Process Model 151–2
    revision 157–8
    sequence 34–6
    sub-sections 36–7
    and time-frames 30–2
    time-scale 36–8

treatment tactics 165–97
    and discomfort 165–70
    see also confrontation; neuro-linguistic
        programming; time-frames; verb
        tenses
'Treatment Triangle' 15–16, *17*, 64, 152,
    158
    see also contract; diagnosis; treatment
        direction
Try Hard driver 10, 110, 116, 149, 160,
    170
    avoiding 61, 119
    clues to 113–14
    non-verbal signals 153
'two-chair work' 155, 175, 186, 192, 193–4,
    196, 202

vectors, transactional 6, 75
verb tenses viii, 104, 165
    and script belief 180–2
    and soft confrontation 177, 178
    and stroking 180–4
visualisation and contract 66, 80, 102–8
    benefits 106–7
    definition 103
    exercise 104–6
    incomplete 107
    preparation for 103
voice shift
    case study 188–9, 190–1
    and impasse 165, 185, 194
    and internal dialogue 184–5, 186,
        188–90
    and positive intention 190–1, 195, 202

wants
    evaluation 91
    and goals 44–5, 65, 88
Ware, Paul 61, 109, 122–3, 137–8
Ware Sequence 51, 122, 137–42, 154–5
    long/short-term 140, 156
    and personality adaptations 137, 138–9,
        139, 140, 141, 156, 159–62
    summary 141
Woollams, S. and Brown, M. 134–5
word patterns, and drivers 118–19
Work Hard counterscript 74, 91
Workaholic (obsessive-compulsive)
        personality 123, 162
    case study 153, 154–7, 160–1
    and confrontation 174
    and contact areas 140
    and injunctions 127
    and Process Model 149, 153, 154–7,
        160–1